ECOLOGY
OF
CARE

ECOLOGY
OF
CARE

*

An Interdisciplinary Analysis

of the Self

and Moral Obligation

*

ROBERT C. FULLER

WESTMINSTER/JOHN KNOX PRESS
LOUISVILLE, KENTUCKY

Book design by Dovetail Art and Design

First edition

Published by Westminster/John Knox Press
Louisville, Kentucky

This book is printed on acid-free paper that meets the American National Standards Institute Z39.48 standard. ∞

PRINTED IN THE UNITED STATES OF AMERICA
9 8 7 6 5 4 3 2 1

Library of Congress Cataloging-in-Publication Data

Fuller, Robert C., 1952–
    Ecology of care : an interdisciplinary analysis of the self and moral obligation / Robert C. Fuller. — 1st ed.
        p.   cm.
    Includes bibliographical references.
    ISBN 0-664-25212-5

    1. Caring—Moral and ethical aspects.   2. Human ecology—Moral and ethical aspects.   3. Self-realization.   4. Natural theology.   5. Religion and science—1946–   I. Title.
BJ1475.F85 1992
170—dc20   91-45296

To my wife, Kathy,
whose care
enables those around her
to flourish

Contents

Introduction:

Who Cares?

✳

WHO CARES? This is a familiar refrain in modern American life. Sometimes it is uttered with an emphasis indignantly placed on the word "who." The message would appear to be "Why should *I* be bothered?" At other times the word "cares" is drawn out, implying that something or someone is surely not worth the bother. Carelessness is a modern character trait that cuts across generational, ethnic, and class lines. It is particularly prevalent in an American society that for several generations has taken pride in its prodigious capacity for creating new and ever more dazzling consumer goods. In our rush to create something new, however, we never have the time to ask what is worth creating. More importantly, we seem never to have the time to care for what we create. We now see the failure of this facet of our national character. Our buildings, roads, cities, and children all suffer from the general carelessness with which modern individuals conduct their lives. The natural environment, too, has been pushed to its limit and is now demanding that we pay the price for our carefree life-styles.

The general carelessness of modern life is reflected in, and in turn perpetuated by, our educational system. A few years ago Ernest Boyer indicted our country's educational system, particularly our colleges, for failing to "help students understand that they are not only autonomous individuals but also members of a human community."[1] As a college teacher I was particularly taken by Boyer's observation. This book is my effort to respond to this cultural need by helping us to understand the human self and its place within the larger scheme of things. If people are to be whole, they must be able to see their world as whole. And, too, they must know what is required for both them and their world to maintain wholeness. In short, we must learn how to care—and care effectively—for those things and processes that support wholeness for ourselves and the larger environments in which we move and have our being. It is in this sense that education must have a pronounced moral dimension. As Boyer correctly noted, Americans "are products of a society in which the call for individual gratification booms forth on every side while the claims of community are weak."[2] My desire is not to combat this societal imbalance with moralistic pronouncements, but to assemble the various academic perspectives that locate the individual's search for gratification within the larger biological, social, moral, and spiritual environments whose lawful structures determine the success of that search.

This book examines just how and why the quest for individual gratification must include a willingness to care for the larger environments within which we hope to sustain productive activity. The course of this discussion is interdisciplinary throughout. My basic argument is that the fullest implications of each individual's relationship to the wider web of life on this planet can be appreciated only from an interdisciplinary perspective. Evolutionary science, developmental psychology, philosophical ethics, and religious reflection must be placed into dialogue with one another if we hope to achieve reasonably secure knowledge about what genuine caring is about. I have tried to avoid any kind of disciplinary imperialism. Each academic discipline introduced into our discussion will be seen to offer a refinement of some important theme or issue that the preceding discipline raised, but did not address in a focused manner. In this way I seek a genuine integration of insights without subsuming any one disciplinary perspective under another, allegedly superior perspective.

Following this pattern, the book begins with the perspective of the natural sciences and locates humans within the broader evolutionary processes that undergird life on this planet. An evolutionary and ecological view makes it clear that the very future of the human species and hence its possibility for continuing to seek "gratification" depend on how well we learn to care for the natural environment. The second chapter looks to psychological science for information concerning the developmental stages and processes that contribute to optimal human growth. Developmental psychology draws our attention to the ways in which the interpersonal environment affects the course of individual life and, somewhat ironically, reveals the great extent to which personal fulfillment is a function of how fully we care for the needs and interests of others. Importantly, both the natural and social sciences delineate what might be called the "objective requirements" of care in that they describe the necessary preconditions of survival, development, and healthy "gratification." The third and fourth chapters build upon these empirical foundations of caring by first developing them into a philosophical discussion of ethics and, finally, into a broadly religious view of the nature and meaning of life. The conclusion situates the issue of care in a social and cultural context that illuminates how the various "helping" professions such as psychotherapy and pastoral counseling might engender a caring orientation to life.

Care, as we shall see, is a partial clue to what gives integrity to human life, and consequently this book seeks to make a contribution to contemporary moral and religious thought. This book will address what scholars refer to as the "crisis" of moral justification in contemporary intellectual thought. The critical tools of modern philosophy have shaken the foundations of ethical thought. Analysis of ethical language and terminology reveal that moral discourse lacks the kind of objective, verifiable "facts" that command authority or produce consensus. Moral judgments are seen to be rooted in a theorist's own subjective biases, and thus it is generally thought to be impossible to construct a rationally compelling ethical theory. Terms such as *good, bad, moral,* and *wrong* are, in this view, little more than subjective preferences and thus fail to convey factual knowledge. Religion has similarly been criticized for its dependence upon scriptural texts that fail to command intellectual authority in a scientific and culturally pluralistic era. Insofar as religious thought fails to build its normative vision upon objectively verifiable information, it lacks the kind of authority needed to shape conduct in the modern world.

In the third and fourth chapters I will sketch out a scholarly rejoinder to modern difficulties with ethical and religious thought. I will do so by reviving many of the insights first advanced by a group of nineteenth-century philosophers commonly known as the "American pragmatists." American pragmatism, particularly the pragmatism of William James, suggests itself as a helpful starting point because it correctly understands human reason in terms of its evolutionary-adaptive heritage. The pragmatists insisted upon viewing human thought and action as an expression of what might be called "practical reason," as opposed to "theoretical reason." To pragmatism, reason is an instrumental faculty whereby individual organisms seek to adapt to their natural and social environments in ways that yield maximum satisfaction. Ethics, then, can be seen as the effort to reflect on how we might best go about caring for ourselves and others in the course of practical, day-to-day living. Viewed in this way, ethical reflection can and must build upon empirical information supplied by the natural and social sciences concerning those forms of conduct that will most likely contribute to the maximum satisfaction of the individual and the larger community of living organisms of which that individual is a part.

What will emerge in this discussion of caring is a sense of the radical interdependence of life on this planet. Responsible care is born of this vision of how fully connected each and every individual is, not only to a larger social community, but to the larger ecosystem within which human existence is both nourished and limited. This view of the web of life on earth is fraught with imagery and insights that are suggestive to the religious imagination. Practical reason is quite naturally tied up with religious thought, but not necessarily with theology. Historically, theologians have assumed that religious doctrines are the source from which we derive our worldviews and notions of ethical responsibility. In sharp contrast, this book will reverse this process and try to tease at least some religious intuitions from the worldview and ethical patterns that are associated with practical reason and its effort to care for life. Whereas theology is constructed on the basis of revealed texts, religious thought is simply the effort to focus upon what might be called the "limit dimension" of common human experience.[3] Theology aims for systematic, internally consistent doctrines that potentially yield exhaustive explanations of human existence. In contrast, religious thought is content with images and metaphors that reveal partial glimpses of the metaphysical (i.e., beyond or overarching the physical) ground out of which physical existence emerges and has its life or being. This book, then, will explore the religious images that appear to be associated with the physical and psychological structures within which humans are lured into caring for themselves and their universe. In this way it seeks to make a direct contribution both to modern religious thought and to what might be called the "cure of souls" tradition that entails issues of spiritual care and guidance.

1

Evolution, Adaptation, and Care

✳

WHO AM I? How did I come into being? What kind of world do I live in? How should I go about living in this world to be sure that I will obtain the highest and best things that life has to offer? These are the kinds of questions that dominate the world's great philosophical and religious traditions. These questions can be broken into a series of smaller parts that can be examined scientifically. Evolutionary biology, for example, has much to say about how various organisms—including humans—came into existence and about the lawful processes that determine an organism's chances of prospering within its habitat. True, evolutionary biology has little light to shed on the most abstract or metaphysical aspects of these great questions about life. It cannot tell us who we are, where we came from, or how we should live in any ultimate or normative sense. But good metaphysics must be grounded in good physics. That is, metaphysics (i.e., the attempt to understand the causal powers and lawful structures that lie beyond, or gave rise to, the created world of physical existence) is only as meaningful for our self-understanding as its empirical foundations enable it to be. And thus, although we cannot expect natural sciences such as evolutionary biology to uncover the First Cause of the universe or the "ultimate" meaning of life, we can expect them to provide us with the best intellectual building blocks that we can reasonably hope for as we set about the task of trying to answer these questions. Evolutionary biology depicts the basic needs that belong to the human individual by virtue of his or her evolutionary heritage and therefore has a direct bearing upon our understanding of how these needs might come together to form a system of values.

The Interdependence of Life

Evolutionary science has made two fundamental contributions that must guide any inquiry into human values.[1] The first is the peculiarly vivid way in which it reveals the interdependence of living beings. The second is its discovery of change and development as intrinsic to the life process and the further discovery that this development is shaped and regulated by the interplay of two principal processes: free variation (mutation) and natural selection.

Evolution is the process whereby life on this planet has gradually developed from the first one-celled organisms into the vast variety of species that we know today. We can postpone "the religious question" of the First Cause or ultimate source of this creative process until chapter 4. For present purposes it is sufficient to note that evolutionary science has given empirical confirmation to one of the most prevalent of all religious intuitions: From the one has come the many. When traced back to their point of origin, the many forms of life on this planet can be seen to have emerged from one creative source. Thus, both scientifically and theologically considered, the history of every species on this planet can be followed back to points of common origin. The renowned biologist George Gaylord Simpson summarized the scientific formulation of this important principle of modern thought by writing that

> the first grand lesson from evolution was that of the unity of life . . .
> all living things are brothers in the very real, material sense that all
> have arisen from one source and been developed within the divergent
> intricacies of one process.[2]

Many of the biological concepts that pertain to the fundamental interdependence of all living organisms are observable features of the present environment and in this sense are not derived from evolutionary perspectives per se. The concepts of "ecosystem" and "food chain," for example, denote the continuous dependence that any one organism or species has upon the existence and functions of other species. Biological systems are such that each organism and species requires materials provided by other organisms and species even as it in turn provides some life-nourishing material to another member of the ecosystem. Much of biology has to do with the study of how "balance" is maintained in any ecosystem and how competition over limited resources serves in the long run to maintain reciprocity and interdependence among living things. Should any one element of a food chain or ecosystem become rendered "unusable" through depletion or detrimental change, there will be an adverse—and possibly lethal—impact upon every other member of that biological system. Thus the interdependence of every organism on this planet not only is the precondition or enabling principle of life but also imposes a rigid limit on the destiny of each species to which it has given rise.

Such biological concepts as food chain and ecosystem might at first glance give the impression of a static system in which the interconnected parts are maintained in a fairly uninterrupted balance or homeostasis. However, evolutionary perspective shows us that nature's system of checks and balances is dynamic and creative in its own right. The web of life on this planet is teeming with the potential to change and express itself in novel forms. The mineral, organic, and animal kingdoms of life are but new orders of expression through which "the one" has over time evolved into "the many." They are successive orders of existence that have arisen within and upon one another. The mechanisms that effect this change and development are the key to explaining the emergence of the human species and, importantly, the key to understanding the place and obligations of humanity within the web of life.

The Laws of Change and Development

The history of life on this planet has been marked by ceaseless transformation. New species come into existence. They often modify over time. Some species become extinct. It is to Charles Darwin that we owe the thanks for educing the fundamental laws that govern these dynamic transformations of life. As a young man, Darwin read with fascination the writings of the British economist Thomas Malthus. Malthus had developed the rather pessimistic thesis that because the human population was growing at an exponential rate, we would eventually outstrip available food supplies and make widespread famine inevitable. According to Malthus, this catastrophe could only be averted if the population were decreased by other factors such as war, disease, or "moral restraint." Darwin was intrigued by Malthus's postulate concerning the exponential growth of populations because he had observed that most natural populations of animals and plants are in fact fairly stable. It became obvious to him that many more individuals are born in any species than ultimately survive. Darwin concluded that the survivors must possess some characteristics that permit them to make use of the limited resources at their disposal, while other members of the species, lacking these same characteristics, simply die. He further realized that the survivors then pass on these survival-oriented characteristics to their offspring. In the meantime, individuals who lacked these characteristics would have fewer or even no offspring. If this process repeated itself for just a few generations, the entire species would gradually be transformed.

It was Darwin's genius to show how this competition or "struggle" for those resources that permit survival serves as the driving force behind the change and development found in nature. As Darwin put it,

> Owing to this struggle, *variations,* however slight and from whatever cause proceeding, if they be in any degree profitable to the individuals of a species, in their infinitely complex relations to other organic beings and to their physical conditions of life, will tend to the preservation of such individuals, and will generally be inherited by the offspring. The offspring, also, will thus have a better chance of surviving, for, of the many individuals of any species which are periodically born, but a small number can survive. I have called this principle, by which each slight variation, if useful, is preserved, by the term *natural selection,* in order to mark its relation to man's power of selection (emphasis added).[3]

Darwin's contribution to evolutionary science, then, was his delineation of free variation, or mutation, and natural selection as the two principal factors that influence the change and development of living things. Darwin lived a few decades too early to be able to understand fully just why and how variation occurs in the realm of nature. It remained for Austrian botanist Gregor Mendel and subsequent generations of researchers to establish a scientific understanding of genetics and to explain how variations or mutations arise in the genetic code that transmits life. The field of genetics has filled in the missing link and thus completed the Darwinian revolution in our understanding of nature's ceaseless transformations. We now know that what is termed a "point mutation" occurs when the DNA sequence of a gene is accidentally altered during the process of replication and the resulting new nucleotide sequence is passed to the offspring. This freely occurring variation in the genetic code happens either when one or more nucleotides are substituted for others in the original sequence, or when one or more nucleotides are added or deleted from that original sequence. This variability in genetic codes, commonly called a mutation, is entirely a matter of chance. That is, at the level of genetic variability, the process that triggers change or development is random and even accidental. It is important to understand that these variations or mutations in the genetic code are essentially a disordering process and occur wholly irrespective of whether they are harmful or beneficial to the organism that inherits these altered genetic codes.

Some changes in the genetic code may be so slight that they neither impair nor improve the organism's ability to function within its environment. These changes will then be passed to subsequent generations and impart some additional variety among members of that species. In many other instances, changes in the genetic code can lead to serious malformation of the organism inheriting the changed DNA and thus impair both its ability to function within its environment and its ability to produce offspring. These genetic mutations will then disappear with the individual organism that possessed them. Occasionally, however, a newly risen mutation may alter the organism's development in such a way as to enhance its ability to adapt successfully to the environment. As Theodosius Dobzhansky and his coauthors point out, "The probability of such an event is greater when organisms colonize a new habitat, or when environmental changes present a population with new challenges. In these cases the adaptation of the population is less than optimal and there is greater opportunity for new mutations to be adaptive."[4]

Natural selection, then, is the process whereby the originally random and accidental genetic changes are either "selected for" or "selected against" by the larger environment. Darwin wrote that "natural selection is daily and hourly scrutinizing, throughout the world, the slightest variations, rejecting those that are bad, preserving and adding up all that are good; silently and insensibly working, whenever and wherever opportunity offers, at the improvement of each organic being in relation to its organic and inorganic conditions of life."[5] Natural selection, by screening out genetic codes that do not enable organisms to compete successfully for limited resources, promotes the adaptation of a species to its environment. What is often called "Darwinian fitness" is the condition of being able to survive and even flourish by taking maximum advantage of the resources within one's environment.

Natural selection thus produces adaptation. This process tends to produce differentiation among species because, as Darwin observed, "the more diversified the descendants from any one species become in structure, constitution and habits, by so much will they be better enabled to seize on many and widely diversified places in the polity of nature, and so be enabled to increase in numbers."[6] Continuing adaptations arise that differentiate species, and "the ultimate result is that each creature tends to become more and more improved in relation to its conditions. This improvement inevitably leads to the greater advancement of the organization of the greater number of living beings throughout the world."[7] Natural selection, or what is sometimes called the "survival of the fittest," does not necessarily include the progressive development of every species. Some species have existed with the same genetic structure for over eighty million years. The measure of Darwinian fitness is whether at a given moment a species is able to survive and successfully generate offspring. Fitness is a quality that is specific to each species and simply pertains to the adequacy with which a particular species is able to take advantage of its own peculiar niche (or polity, as Darwin so eloquently put it) in the overall environment. Thus, for example, the cockroach is every bit as "fit" as the human in terms of adaptedness to the environmental challenges it must be able to surmount en route to successfully generating offspring.

The "struggle for existence" is thus not necessarily a combative struggle in the sense of one species or individual doing battle with another (although it might include this). This struggle has instead to do with each species' own "trial and error" attempts to maintain a balance of nature, to make more efficient use of available food, to care better for its young, to eliminate intragroup discord, and to control better the destructive consequences of unrestrained aggression. For this reason natural selection should be thought of not only in a negative way (i.e., eliminating inferior gene groups) but also in terms of its positive function of favoring gene combinations that enhance a species' capacity for ongoing adaptedness to the environment. It is in this sense that such preeminent evolutionary theorists as Dobzhansky, Francisco Ayala, Julian Huxley, and George Gaylord Simpson have all called natural selection "creative." Although mutations are themselves "blind" in the sense of being chance alterations with no foresight of their consequences, natural selection represents the cumulative trend of changes tending toward higher levels of organization that include, among others, the deepening of sentience and the emergence of thought.

It is important to keep in mind that evolutionary change occurs in the genetic code existing within populations and not in the acquired behaviors exhibited by individuals. Characteristics and traits acquired during an organism's lifetime have no influence upon the genetic code that will be transmitted to offspring. As Dobzhansky and his coauthors have put it, "From the evolutionary point of view the individual is ephemeral; only populations persist through time. The continuity derives from the mechanism of biological heredity."[8] Each population or species has its evolutionary origin and, as dictated by natural selection, its own evolutionary fate. Unlike individual organisms, species do not have a fixed life span and may, in fact, continue indefinitely so long as the environment does not change in such a way as to render it ill-adapted or so long as no adverse mutations occur to any unusually large degree. Simpson makes this issue clear in his explanation that the death of a species "is not a fate implanted within the racial tissues as inevitable old age and death are implanted in the tissues of individuals, but is again a phenomenon explicable only on the basis of the complex material interaction of populations on their environment."[9]

The birth and death of species are thus the ebb and flow through which the web of life expresses itself. In the evolutionary perspective, the birth and death of species are not really things that can be called "good" or "bad" but are rather phases by which new harmonies and new forms of adaptedness arise out of the dynamic flux of life. As Simpson puts it, the extinction of any race or species "merely reflects the rate of progressive change. A short life span for any one type means not that death soon overtook it but that life rapidly carried it on to other forms of being."[10] Variation and natural selection are facts of natural existence, and there is, finally, no more reason to approve or disapprove of them than such other lawful constants as gravity or the forward progression of time. Douglas Futuyama puts this well in his remark that

> in the world of nature, there is neither good nor evil. The extinction of a comet astronomers recently sighted plunging into the sun is not a cosmic tragedy, it is just an event produced by mindless physical forces. Neither is the extinction of the pterodactyl tragic, nor is the struggle for existence that causes evolution either good or bad. It just is. Species arise throughout the ages, "but time and chance happeneth to them all."[11]

Futuyama's remark is a bit blunt and perhaps overstates the "mindless-ness" of physical reality. But it does underscore the impersonal process of natural selection and its unremitting role in selecting against those species that do not remain in a condition of ongoing adaptedness to their larger environment.

Humanity's Place in the Web of Life

Prior to Darwin it was widely believed that humans had a unique and privileged place in the universe. In the Bible of Judaism and Christianity, the very purpose of creation is the placing of Adam and Eve in their garden paradise. Darwin's theoretical breakthrough has made it impossible for educated people to continue to maintain such a naive affirmation of humanity's privileged role in the universe. Evolution shows clearly that instead of being created ex nihilo to preside over the whole of creation, humanity is but one of the countless numbers of species produced by the interplay of variation and natural selection. The message of evolution is that we are not unique, if by that we mean that humans are somehow separate from the rest of creation.

The genetic variations that are the driving mechanism of evolution occur in random, capricious ways. There is, then, no overall goal, purpose, or direction to the evolution of life per se. As Simpson puts it, "Evolution is not invariably accompanied by progress, nor does it really seem to be characterized by progress as an essential feature."[12] There has, of course, been progress within evolution if by that we mean that each species displays its own successive line of increasing range and variety of adjustments to its environment. Every species evidences progress of this sort, and the concept of progress in this sense would therefore depend on the peculiar species one is considering at the moment. That is, there is no standard according to which uniform progress can be said to have occurred in the overall evolution of life. Teleology, the attempt to explain the origin and existence of something in terms of the purpose or goal it eventually serves, can be applied to evolution only in an indeterminate sense. Dobzhansky and his colleagues explain that

> although there are teleologically determinate processes in the living world, like embryological development and physiological homeosta-sis, the evolutionary origin of living beings is teleological only in the indeterminate sense. Natural selection does not in any way direct evolution toward any particular organism or toward any particular properties.[13]

Realizing that evolution in no way "intended" the human species and that the human species cannot truly be said to have "progressed" more than any other species in terms of fitting into the overall ecosystem on this planet, it is still possible to look at the kinds of progress that happened along the particular evolutionary line that has expressed itself in humans. Simpson writes, "To man, evolutionary change in the direction of man is progress, of this particular sort. It is not progress in a general or objective sense and does not warrant choice of the line of man's ancestry as the central line of evolution as a whole."[14] G. Ledyard Stebbins, for example, sees in the evolution of the human species a bias toward increased complexity of organization.[15] Francisco Ayala argues that human evolution displays a general bias toward enhanced abilities to gather and process information about the environment.[16] Both of these hypotheses concerning a potential bias of natural selection in the direction that humans now inhabit are consistent with a more general observation concerning the directional activity of life on this planet. Our sciences reveal that what we call life is a system of order that maintains and even increases this order in a physical environment that is otherwise characterized by decreasing order.[17] The evolution of life on this planet runs in a direction opposite that of the second law of thermodynamics. This is, of course, not to suggest that the evolutionary process truly violates the second law of thermodynamics, which maintains that order inevitably decreases in any closed physical system. Yet it remains true that life as we know it is defined by its ability to maintain and even increase order. Humanity's possession of genetic traits that permit an increased complexity of organization and increased information-processing ability would seem to be consistent with this fundamental characteristic of life as an order-increasing system. Thus, although natural selection did not intend humans in any predetermined sense, it does indeed favor order-producing and order-maintaining systems in ways that make the genetic material found in humans especially "fit."

Whatever the particular biases (if any) of natural selection, it is clear that, in humans, evolution gave rise to an intricately developed central nervous system that is coordinated by a brain with an unprecedentedly large cerebral cortex. This cerebral cortex permits tremendous flexibility in an organism's interaction with the environment. Humans, who have inherited a massive array of instinctual tendencies and genetically determined predispositions, are nonetheless quite "plastic" in that their large cerebral cortex makes it possible to override reflexive responses to environmental stimuli and to substitute others instead. In his epochal work *On Aggression,* Konrad Lorenz made the implications of this plasticity in human behavior clear by noting that "man's whole system of innate activities and reactions is phylogenetically so constructed, so 'calculated' by evolution, as to *need* to be complemented by cultural tradition (emphasis added)."[18] Cultural tradition, education, the socialization process, and so on all serve to impart direction to human behavior and to assist the individual organism in adapting to its social as well as its natural environment.

What makes human behavior so distinct from that of other species is what Edward O. Wilson describes as the fact that in humans "genes have given away most of their sovereignty" to the patterning that culture provides the organism.[19] The significance of this fact can hardly be overstated. Culture adds a new dimension to the evolutionary process, a dimension that in many respects supersedes the natural selection of genes in favor of the long-term functional value of the ideas, myths, rituals, and behavioral norms that are created and transmitted by culture. Nothing in the previous history of life on this planet even remotely compares to human culture in terms of its rapid ability to invent new forms of life (mutations) and immediately test them for their capacity to enhance life (natural selection). For humans, then, change and development take place through the social and cultural transmission of genes. Simpson contrasts the organic and cultural modes of evolution:

> Organic evolution rejects acquired characters in inheritance and adaptively orients the essentially random, non-environmental inter-play of genetical systems. The *new evolution peculiar to man operates directly by* the inheritance of acquired characters, of knowledge and *learned activities* which arise in and are continuously a part of an organismic-environmental system, that of social organization (emphasis added).[20]

There are numerous implications of the emergence of "higher order" cognitive capacities in humans and the simultaneous emergence of social organizations that transmit vast quantities of acquired behavior-shaping information from generation to generation. In fact, the rest of this book will concern itself with the far-reaching implications that this evolutionary emergence has for understanding the laws of change and development for humans and, therefore, for how humans must care for one another. One such consequence of humanity's advanced cognitive skills is that we possess a rich subjective life that prompts us to value and receive satisfaction from a wide range of experiences and activities. William James was one of the first to draw attention to the creative role that humanity's "subjective interests" have in shaping human existence when he argued that, for humans, "survival is only one out of many interests— primus inter pares, perhaps, but still in the midst of peers."[21] Humans also seek out ever new forms of activity that contribute to what James called the "subjective richness" of life. We actively pursue social affection, play, aesthetic pleasure, religious emotion, wit, and philosophical contemplation. Moreover, we seek these not for their survival value but simply for their ability to enrich our subjective experience. As James pointed out, those individuals who contribute to this enhancement of the subjective sphere of human experience through their intellectual or artistic abilities are generally prized and rewarded by the larger social group and in this way prove to have a form of "fitness" even though they might well be ill-adapted to survival in a purely physical environment.

A second implication of the emergence of inherited cultural patterns (which Richard Dawkins calls "memes" to distinguish this nongenetic code that influences humanity's evolution from genes) is that it makes possible a far more significant role for individuals in the evolutionary process. In organic evolution, as we have seen, the individual is not really the unit of evolutionary change. Genetic variations may occur within a newly developing organism, but true evolutionary change must await the process of natural selection working over several generations. The social dimension of human evolution makes it possible for individuals to have a more pronounced, and a more immediate, impact upon the course of life. Cultural change, as William James noted, is "due to the accumulated influences of individuals, of their examples, their initiative, and their decisions."[22] James pointed out that the relation of the wider culture to the individual is similar to the relation of the natural environment to a "variation" in the Darwinian system. The environment adopts or rejects, preserves or destroys—in short, it selects for or against the individual's initiatives. "The mutations of societies, then, from generation to generation, are in the main due directly or indirectly to the acts or the examples of individuals whose genius was so adapted to the receptivities of the moment, or whose accidental position of authority was so critical that they became ferments, initiators of movement, setters of precedent or fashion, centres of corruption, or destroyers of other persons, whose gifts, had they had free play, would have led society in another direction."[23]

Other such implications of humanity's greater cerebral cortex and its need for a cultural environment will emerge in later discussions. We might anticipate these further implications by briefly pondering why there was such strong selective pressure for the web of life to have given rise to such a developed thinking capacity. Nothing ever "just happens" in the process of natural selection. Michael Ruse has summarized the evolutionary-adaptive rationale for the emergence of humanity's cognitive powers by writing that

> it seems fairly clear that cooperation was a significant factor in human prehistory as our ancestors roamed the plains of Africa hunting, gathering, and scavenging especially on the carcasses of large mammals. Large mammals represent a valuable source of protein; thus, the intelligence required to pinpoint and utilize them properly would be of great adaptive value in life's struggles.[24]

Ruse's account is important in that it links the capacity for higher order thinking with the evolutionary-adaptive requirement of cooperation. The evolution of humans required mutual caring. It is in this sense that Theodosius Dobzhansky and his colleagues assert that humans are genetically determined "ethicizing beings." "The evolutionary development that made the ascent of man possible has not endowed mankind with any particular system of ethics; it has, however, made human beings capable of learning various kinds of ethics, values, and morals."[25] The plasticity of human existence not only makes humans capable of learning some set of values, it requires them to learn some such set of culturally transmitted behavioral codes.

The cognitive capacities peculiar to humans do make the place of humans in the web of life unique, even if not privileged or in some way especially prized. Simpson describes this unique place fairly succinctly: "Man, alone among all organisms, knows that he evolves and he alone is capable of directing his own evolution."[26] If humans are unique, then, it is because our brains, tongues, and hands permit us to accumulate knowledge, to build upon the experience of previous generations, and to anticipate the future. If we are unique in the universe, according to Colin Patterson, it is "in the sense that we are our own master, and have no one to blame but ourselves, for if the future is anywhere it is in our heads."[27]

The place of humanity in the evolutionary process is one of tremendous possibility and tremendous responsibility. It remains to be seen whether this awareness of our responsibility for the future of life on this planet will elicit from us a new spiritual and moral strength. There is, as Julian

Huxley so confidently proclaimed, a certain grandeur in the evolutionary view of human nature, a grandeur that might potentially inspire us to new levels of self-understanding and inspired action.

> In the light of evolutionary biology man can now see himself as the sole agent of further evolutionary advance on this planet. . . . He finds himself in the unexpected position of business manager for the cosmic process of evolution. He no longer ought to feel separated from the rest of nature, for he is part of it—that part which has become conscious, capable of love and understanding and aspiration.[28]

The Genetic Foundations of Care

Darwin anticipated potential objections to his theory of the role that mutations and natural selection play in creating the various species found in nature. One of these possible difficulties was the presence of sterile castes in many social insects. It might reasonably be argued that the existence of such sterile castes disproves the operation of natural selection because genetic changes producing sterility ought to reduce these organism's chances of survival; by definition, sterile organisms do not generate offspring and hence it would appear that they could not have evolved through natural selection. Darwin, however, realized that sterility in some members of the colony might indeed serve an adaptive function for the colony as a whole. He reasoned that if sterile insects perform essential tasks for the colony such as food-gathering and protection, they simultaneously contribute to the success of the total colony's gene pool by making it possible for the fertile insects to spend all of their energies on reproduction. Because the sterility of some members of the gene pool contributes significantly to the chances of the colony's ability to produce offspring, then sterility of some individuals would actually be "selected for" in the process of natural selection. Darwin referred to this process as "family selection." Darwin's point here was that sterility of some individuals could be favored if that sterility was compensated by the extra number of offspring surviving to his or her relatives. For example, the sterile female workers in a honeybee colony are usually full sisters of the few fertile bees who will insure the colony's reproduction. In a colony containing tens of thousands of members, it will not really matter whether some of these sterile workers are lost as they sting potential predators. What matters from the standpoint of natural selection is that the fertile members of the colony remain safe to insure the colony's reproductive future.

Darwin's first hints concerning family selection have given rise to a field of study that is generally referred to as sociobiology.[29] Sociobiology uses insights from evolutionary biology to study and explain the social behavior of various species. It is an empirical fact that animals, often of different species, actually work together and cooperate for their mutual benefit. What most intrigues researchers in sociobiology are those instances, such as the sterile honeybee, in which this cooperation may be at a considerable cost to the individual. Cooperative behavior of this sort is called *altruism*—the risking of one's own personal fitness for the good of another. In this biological sense, of course, the concept of altruism does not imply any conscious intention or desire to do good on the part of the "sacrificing" individual. Instead, altruism is here understood as an adaptive behavior controlled by the DNA in genes to help ensure the species' capacity to reproduce these genes. In his important text *Sociobiology: The New Synthesis,* Edward O. Wilson explains that in order to understand social behavior from the evolutionary point of view you must be able to comprehend that "the organism is only DNA's way of making more DNA."[30] Understood this way, much of what biologists call "altruistic" behavior is actually the epitome of genetic selfishness. Put bluntly, the process of natural selection frequently favors short-sighted selfishness. At particular points in their evolutionary history, various species have found it adaptively useful to favor kin at the expense of others, practice infanticide, engage in cannibalism, and commit "altruistic" suicide. It should be readily apparent that our capacity for ethics, while born of our evolutionary heritage, must ultimately be expanded from its initial predisposition toward short-term advantage to encompass the longer-term needs of the larger environment.

Recent evolutionary studies have given rise to several models that help explain altruistic behavior. The kind of altruism in which an individual performs an action that decreases its own fitness but in so doing greatly enhances the reproductive abilities of its relatives is known as "kin selection."[31] Another kind, "reciprocal altruism," refers to the many instances in nature in which the offering of help or assistance at one point tends to secure similar help for oneself in the future ("I'll scratch your back if you'll scratch mine").[32] These and other sociobiological concepts have helped explain a variety of puzzling phenomena throughout the animal kingdom. And, importantly, these biological explanations of altruistic social behavior also help us to understand more precisely the evolutionary-adaptive functions of human care and ethics.

Among all the species that populate this earth, humans are almost uniquely in need of "altruism." As Ruse explains, a human being alone would be virtually helpless.

> We have neither weapons of attack nor means of defense. We are not
> particularly mobile nor particularly agile. We are neither too large to
> threaten nor too small to be overlooked. Thus, we need each other to
> survive and reproduce, and others need us.[33]

For humans, altruism is a precondition of survival. Although our
altruistic impulses, beliefs, and moral ideas are genetically controlled
propensities, they do not control human behavior as rigidly as would be
found in the social insects. Nevertheless, we have surely inherited a
genetic core that imparts certain innate dispositions that guide our actions
and structure our thinking processes. The general effect of these genetically encoded controls on our behavior is to give us, at the deepest level of
feeling and motivation, a fundamental sense that we ought to help each
other. Darwin emphasized that, "In order that primeval men, or the
ape-like progenitors of man should become social, they must have
acquired the same general disposition [of sympathy]. They would have
felt uneasy when separated from their comrades, for whom they would
have felt some degree of love; they would have warned each other of
danger, and have given mutual aid in attack or defense. All this implies
some degree of sympathy, fidelity, and courage. . . . Selfish and
contentious people will not cohere, and without coherence nothing can be
effected."[34]

Jeffrie Murphy has conveniently summarized Darwin's view of the origin
of social instincts in human beings and has drawn attention to the fact that
the survival of human beings required that people care for each other in
ways that, if not exactly moral, at least form the basis of moral caring.

> Care only for self, or even care limited to one's immediate family,
> would not have been sufficient. Survival required a more generalized
> caring for all members of one's community and, as the communities
> became more complex, for the rules establishing duties within the
> communities. Advanced or civilized morality, then, is not the
> artificial creation, *ex nihilo*, of something totally new. It is, rather,
> simply an increasingly disinterested and abstracted generalization of
> the primitive caring that insured the survival of human beings.[35]

Darwin was quick to observe that the theory of natural selection can
account for the origin of our fundamental tendency to care, but that it can
not wholly explain the rationally reflected ethical principles that have
been generated in human history. Humans' capacity for communication,
abstract thought, and the use of symbols make culture the prime force
shaping our ethical systems. Darwin wrote, "With civilised nations, as far
as an advanced standard of morality, and an increased number of fairly
good men are concerned, natural selection apparently effects but little;

though the fundamental social instincts were originally thus gained. . . . The moral nature of man has reached its present standard, partly through the advancement of his reasoning powers and consequently of a just public opinion, but especially from his sympathies having been rendered more tender and widely diffused through the effects of habit, example, instruction, and reflection."[36]

While Darwin's theory of natural selection shed important light on the origin and diffusion of a caring or altruistic sentiment among humans, it tells us little about the actual use, misuse, or failure to use that sentiment. The evolutionary development that made humanity's ascent possible gave us a genetically endowed capacity for ethical thought, but did not give us any specific system of ethics. Particular systems of ethics evolve in the process of cultural interaction. Human beings, with all our proclivities to selfishness and hedonism, are nonetheless educable. This educability permits us to counteract these proclivities through group ethics derived from culture. Natural selection for educability and plasticity of behavior, not for genetically determined egoism or altruism, has dominated human evolution.[37]

To summarize, both reason and culture play a large role in the development of the ethical theories that translate our desire to care into specific actions. To the degree that rational deliberation or cultural education form a part of a person's moral world, then to that same degree the person's behavior is not biologically determined in the strictest sense. Reason serves our altruistic impulses by providing an instrumental faculty that allows human beings to compare present experiences with past experiences and to anticipate the future.[38] In this way reason introduces deliberate planning, through trial and error, into our efforts to insure personal and community survival.

Yet, in conclusion, the human need to care and to be cared for is very much rooted in our evolutionary heritage. Care or altruistic behavior is in many respects what has made the human species biologically possible. The survival of our species is thus dependent upon this evolutionary-adaptive trait. We also have much to learn from evolutionary theory about the biological functions this trait serves. We must, for example, learn to recognize and guard against the tendency for natural selection to promote selfish, overly aggressive, or short-sighted behavior. For example, numerous species seek to protect their kin or group through some form of "boundary creation" and "boundary maintenance." In humans this same tendency underlies the kind of group loyalty that is likely to promote bigotry, prejudice, and stubborn refusal to coexist peacefully with those outside one's own group. Such selfish and short-sighted forms of adaptation are contributing causes of the most poignant symbol of modern carelessness—the threat of the nuclear destruction of our planet.

The ability of evolutionary biology to illuminate both the problems and the promises of our genetic heritage prompted Edward O. Wilson to argue that "scientists and humanists should consider together the possibility that the time has come for ethics to be removed temporarily from the hands of the philosophers and biologized."[39] Wilson argues that we now require "a biology of ethics," which will make possible the selection of a more deeply understood and enduring code of moral values.[40] Because human ethical behavior is not fully biologically determined, a fully biologized ethics is not possible. But by the same token, our genetic inheritance imparts the possibilities and limitations of our behavior. And we must, of course, behave in ways that maintain an adaptedness to our biological environment.[41] For this reason no sensible system of human ethics can be constructed that does not rest firmly upon "biologized" foundations.

The Urgent Need for a Deep Ecology

Adaptation is an ongoing process. Both short-term fluctuations in the environment and long-term, nonreversing environmental trends impose new selective pressures that favor evolutionary change. In the case of humans this whole process is quite complex because humans themselves are frequently the agents of environmental change. Human culture has gradually given rise to ranges of behavior (e.g., scientific, industrial, and technological achievements) that actually transform the natural environment in ever-new ways. These changes in turn exert selective pressures that spur on yet a new round of cultural change. What remains to be seen, however, is whether the changes that humans have introduced into their environment are changes that will be "selected for" in the long-term operation of natural selection. That is, much of our modern technology, industrial practices, and life-styles are in the final analysis mutations or free variations that have appeared in the human species. It is not at all clear whether these free variations will increase humanity's adaptedness to the larger ecosystem or are instead generating irreversible processes that will make our extinction imminent.

For more than 99.9 percent of the time that humans have inhabited the earth they were hunters and gatherers, obtaining food by gathering edible wild plants and hunting wild game and fish from the immediate vicinity.[42] Archaeological evidence suggests that throughout this long period humans lived in small tribes of about fifty people who worked together to secure enough food to survive. Because of their small numbers, these humans had little impact on their environment. Their culture helped them to compensate for their relative weakness and lack of agility and, as a cooperative unit, they were able to prosper as a species for thousands upon thousands of years in a balanced or homeostatic relationship with the larger ecosystem.

Around 8000 B.C. humans began to domesticate wild animals and began primitive farming. Full agriculture emerged about 5000 B.C. with the invention of the metal plow, which greatly increased crop productivity and made it possible for humans to provide a dependable and sufficient source of food. The world population began to increase owing to the larger, dependable food supply. For the first time humans began to shape the surface of the earth to suit their needs by clearing larger areas of land for farming and for the emerging villages and towns. A class of skilled craftsmen developed in these towns and traded the goods they produced for the surplus food now produced by farmers. The rise of these agriculture-based urban societies had an environmental impact that far exceeded the impact of the hunting and gathering societies that preceded them. Forests were cut down and grasslands were either plowed up or converted to grazing pastures. The massive land clearing endangered numerous forms of plant and animal life. The cleared areas also contributed to soil erosion, and the silt that washed off these stripped areas polluted streams, rivers, and lakes. The wastes produced by large numbers of urban dwellers created its own problems, including the spread of infectious diseases and parasites. As G. Tyler Miller describes this process, "The development and gradual spread of agriculture meant that most of the earth's population shifted from life as hunter-gatherers *in nature* to life as shepherds, farmers, and urban dwellers *against nature*. For the first time, human beings saw themselves as distinct and apart from the rest of nature, and they created the concepts of 'wild' and 'wilderness' to apply to animals, plants, and parts of the earth not [yet] under their control."[43]

With the advent of the Industrial Revolution in the early nineteenth century, humanity's efforts to subjugate the remaining wilderness escalated with a vengeance. By the middle of the twentieth century, 33 of the planet's 166 nations utilized the energy of fossil fuels and the industrial advances made possible by modern science and technology to create economies that bear almost no resemblance to the conditions in which humans lived just eight or ten generations earlier. Those humans fortunate enough to have been born in one of the thirty-three developed countries during the past sixty years have been surrounded by an ever-increasing rate of agricultural productivity, an industrial system capable of making useful and affordable products with which to ease the work associated with day-to-day living, a significant increase in the standard of living in terms of per capita income, and a sharp rise in average life expectancy as a result of improvements in medicine, nutrition, and sanitation. The many advantages of life in an advanced industrial era are, however, matched by the intensification of the environmental problems spawned by human culture. Problems associated with (1) the world's continuing population growth, (2) the unequal distribution of wealth which thereby creates unprecedented gaps between the "haves" and the "have nots," (3) resource depletion, and (4) pollution are terrifying testimonials to the carelessness with which modern humans have sought to adapt to their environment.

It took the human species between two and five million years to reach a total population of one billion. During that time the population grew at the rate of about 0.002 percent per year. Yet, because of increased agricultural productivity and advanced industrial techniques, the annual growth rate of the population increased drastically, and it took only 130 years to add the second billion humans. It took only an additional 30 years to reach a population of three billion, 15 years for the next billion, and only 12 years for the fifth billion. The world's population now grows at the rate of 1.7 million people per week (9,900 per hour). What further accentuates this "population bomb" is the fact that the vast bulk of this population growth has taken place in urban areas and thereby further contributed to the kinds of pollution, resource depletion, and social tension that accompany the overcrowding of a population. We are now perilously close to what biologist Garrett Hardin calls the "carrying capacity" of any ecosystem—the population limit beyond which that species cannot be sustained by the fixed resources needed to sustain life in a given environment.

Connected with the rapid growth in the population during the past few hundred years has been the sustained division of the world into the "more developed" (33 of the 166 countries on this planet) and the "less developed" (representing 133 countries and, of course, those people beneath the poverty line in the 33 more-developed countries) societies. At present, 92 percent of the world's annual population growth is taking place within the least economically developed societies. Thus, although the world is able to feed more people than ever before, at least one out of every six human beings is too poor to buy enough food to survive. Between twelve million and twenty million people die every year due to starvation or malnutrition. Countless others linger on in abject poverty, enduring an existence that is virtually without hope. It is interesting to note that the world economy has become so international that at long last persons in the more developed nations have become aware of their interconnectedness with these desperate people. The potential threat of these lesser developed nations defaulting on their enormous loans has finally engaged the self-interest of the world's affluent population and made it attentive to both the plight of the underprivileged and the possibly disastrous consequences to everyone if a way of responsibly caring for this situation is not soon discovered.

The world's increased population has also accelerated the rate at which we have been depleting the earth's resources. Soil and water, for example, are potentially renewable resources. However, our indiscriminate and careless use of these resources is now threatening the biological integrity of numerous species, including humans. Soil is the base of all nonaquatic life and provides the nutrients of the entire biosphere. Our topsoil, the fertile material from which organic life proceeds, is now eroding faster than it can be formed. Soil erosion, wind, grazing, logging, construction, and pollution are seriously jeopardizing the base out of which life emerges. Of all the water on earth, only 0.5% is available as fresh water in rivers, lakes, and recoverable underground deposits. This is simply an insufficient amount to sustain the populations that are projected to be inhabiting earth in just a few generations. The continuous contamination of our water supplies exacerbates this crisis. All life as we know it requires uncontaminated sources of water, and hence humanity has already put strains into earth's environmental balance that, if not addressed, will begin "selecting against" organisms that cannot find steady access to uncontaminated water.

Such nonrenewable resources as mineral deposits, crude oil, shale oil, natural gas, and coal are already in severely diminished supply. For example, the U.S. Department of Energy and the American Petroleum Institute estimate that 80 percent of the world's known resources of crude oil will be depleted by the year 2013. Shale oil deposits will be exhausted by 2032, and the world's natural gas reserves will be depleted by 2033. At our present consumption rate we will run out of coal in less than three hundred years. Human industrialized society has thus approached the point where it has consumed the very energy resources that made it possible in the first place. We have created so much that it has become impossible to sustain our own creations.

The horrors of worldwide pollution succeed in making daily headlines even if they fail to prick the conscience of the citizens of the world's most developed nations. Oil spills and chemical runoff have contaminated our water, directly destroyed numerous forms of wildlife, and are annihilating the phytoplankton that renews much of the oxygen in the atmosphere. Industrial pollutants threaten to warm the earth's atmosphere, melt the polar ice caps, and play havoc with the weather and growing seasons. The intensive use of petrochemical fertilizers might well be exhausting the topsoil even as they contaminate our supply of fresh water. And, finally, the indiscriminate disposal of nuclear waste threatens the genetic integrity of every living being on this planet. Radioactive waste can cause massive chromosomal mutations and greatly accelerate the growth of cancer.

Spent fuel rods from nuclear power plants must be stored safely for at least ten thousand years before they decay to acceptable levels of radioactivity. It is thus rather frightening to realize that over four thousand of these rods are being added to our nuclear waste each year and that radioactive liquid wastes equal in volume to about two hundred Olympic-size pools currently await permanent storage. There is still no accepted solution of how to dispose of radioactive materials safely, and thus with each passing day we increase our risk of serious and irreversible environmental damage.

It is, then, only in the most recent years of humanity's history on this planet that we have developed in sufficient numbers, acquired enough power, and so thoughtlessly conducted ourselves that we now threaten the biological base upon which every living organism depends. The environmental or ecological movement that has gained momentum during the past twenty years has tried to educate modern people concerning the disastrous consequences of our general carelessness. In particular, it has become clear that we will not be able to solve our environmental crisis by coming up with an endless series of ad hoc remedies to each new catastrophe. We need, rather, a new and widespread attitude toward nature in which we operate with a higher regard for the biological system within which we function. An early voice in the ecological movement, Aldo Leopold, put this as clearly as any when he argued that we need a "land ethic" to strengthen our moral vision.

> All ethics so far evolved rest upon a single premise: that the individual is a member of a community of interdependent parts. His instincts prompt him to compete for his place in that community, but his ethics prompt him also to co-operate (perhaps in order that there may be a place to compete for). The land ethic simply enlarges the boundaries of the community to include soils, water, plants, and animals, or collectively, the land.[44]

Those who have taken up Leopold's cause have come to call their vision of life a "deep ecology" to contrast it with the simple, reflexive approach to the environment that our governmental agencies use when they merely respond to those ecological crises that can no longer be ignored.[45] Deep ecology is not only born of scientific insight into our biological "rootedness" in the larger ecosystem, but is also anchored in a spiritual sensitivity that intuits a certain ultimacy or sacredness about nature. A deep ecology awakens activity and care because it opens up a sense of fundamental connectedness between each living organism and that ultimate creative force from which all life derives. Thus, to desecrate the environment is a kind of sacrilege.

The term "deep ecology" signifies a certain perspective that humans must adopt if life as we know it is to continue on this planet. Evolutionary science is capable of providing at least some initial hints as to how we might go about understanding the role of humans in the greater scheme of life. Dobzhansky and his coauthors have argued that there are at least three "evolutionary guidelines" for addressing those ecological and cultural problems that threaten the future of evolution on this planet.

> First, the urgency of the situation requires that cultural rather than genetic solutions be sought. Second, the basis for improvement must be the flexibility and diversity of cultural traits, comparable to the genetic flexibility and diversity that exist in populations of animals. Third, the drastic alterations in the human environment that have taken place in very recent times require equally drastic reorganization of human standards and goals. Exploitation, expansion and aggression must be replaced by conservation, population control, and tolerance. Finally, societies cannot advance toward improved conditions without considering, in addition to standards that are technological, ethical standards that are strictly human in nature.[46]

When we ask, then, "Who cares?" a partial answer must be, "Anyone who is concerned with the survival of life on this planet." Evolutionary biology shows us, furthermore, that our efforts to care must take a particular form. Simpson has suggested that we can no longer view the relationship of the individual organism to the larger environment in reductionist terms of any sort. In contrast to reductionist interpretations of life, Simpson suggests a "compositionist" approach that interprets "in terms of the adaptive usefulness of structures and processes to the whole organism and to the species of which it is a part, and still further, in terms of ecological function in the communities in which the species occurs."[47] The compositionist view of judging the worth of any particular course of action has a built-in corrective against the kind of carelessness that is now plaguing modern society. And, as we shall see in chapter 3, it also provides the nucleus of a modern ethic of care.

2

The Self: Agency and Mutuality Through the Life Cycle

*

WE BEGAN THE FIRST CHAPTER with a series of questions that both intrigue and perplex the human species: Who am I? How did humans come into existence? What kind of world do I live in? How should I go about obtaining the best things that life has to offer? The first chapter showed how the natural sciences, particularly evolutionary biology, can shed light on important dimensions of these questions. Evolutionary science teaches us about the radical interdependence of life on this planet, about our origins amidst the "struggle" for existence, and that our future as a species depends on how well we learn to use our adaptive capacities for cooperation and care. The social sciences are also able to help us understand aspects of human identity and the developmental processes whereby individuals change and grow in their pursuit of well-being. This is particularly true of developmental psychology. Developmental psychology focuses on the individual's gradual acquisition of adaptive abilities and therefore offers an additional perspective on how we might best construct and sustain a world suited to human fulfillment.

We have seen that biological adaptation requires a delicate balance between the individual organism and its environment. On the one hand, if the individual organism is to be "selected for" and to survive, it must continually adapt or adjust itself to the limiting conditions imposed by the environment. On the other hand, the organism must also possess the ability to alter its environment and actively shape it in ways that will render it more hospitable and nurturing. Successful adaptation, then, requires a certain balance between (1) the adaptive behaviors whereby individuals seek to adjust themselves to fit the environment and (2) the adaptive behaviors whereby individuals seek to master the environment and reshape it in ways that yield greater satisfaction. This is particularly true in the case of humans. The entire course of the human life span can be interpreted in terms of each person's development of psychological

34

structures that permit that person to balance these two adaptive strategies. Psychological theorists have used different terminology to describe these dual adaptive modalities. David Bakan, for example, has used the concepts of agency and communion.[1] Agency here is meant to refer to a person's efforts to master the environment through self-initiated actions. Communion refers to a person's attempt to adapt through receptivity and by becoming part of a greater whole. Andras Angyal designated these dual modalities as the tendencies toward autonomy and homonomy.[2] As Angyal explains, in the first tendency a person struggles for centrality, trying to control the objects and events of the world. In the second tendency, the person seeks to surrender to and become an organic part of something perceived as greater than oneself.

> The superindividual unit of which one feels oneself a part . . . may be represented for a person by a social unit—family, clan, nation—by a cause, by an ideology, or by a meaningfully ordered universe. *In the realm of aesthetic, social, and moral attitudes this basic human tendency has a central significance.* Its clearest manifestation, however, is in the religious attitude and religious experience (emphasis added).[3]

Arthur Deikman used the terms "activity" and "receptivity" to demarcate the different modes in which the brain structures sensory impressions.[4] Robert Ornstein's *The Psychology of Consciousness* took Deikman's model one step further and suggested that these two modes of cognitive activity are directed by the two hemispheres of the brain.[5] According to this somewhat simplistic view of the cortical division of brain functions, the left hemisphere of the brain actively structures experience in logical ways that best permit a person to manipulate the environment and assure biological survival. The right hemisphere is thought to be more "receptive" and enables people to understand life in more holistic, spatial, and relational ways.

The important point in all of this is that our effort to understand the course of human development must be sensitive to the need for people to achieve both active mastery of the environment (agency) and to find themselves a part of a larger whole (mutuality). Various stages or moments throughout the course of life witness a preponderance of one of these psychological modalities over the other. Yet, on the whole, happiness and fulfillment require a certain reciprocity between the two. And, as we shall see, what best unites these two psychological modalities in ways that enable our personal agency to strengthen, rather than diminish, the final meaning of our personal lives is the virtue of care. By being attentive to the interplay of agency and mutuality throughout the course of human life we will also appreciate what developmental psychology—like evolutionary science—teaches us about the radical interdependence of life in the social ecosystem and how the meaning or integrity of our lives as individuals depends on how well we utilize our capacities for agency in caring ways.

The Self in Developmental Perspective

Psychologists suggest that it is helpful to view human development as proceeding through a series of stages in which these two adaptive modalities are continually developed and reorganized. The concept of "stages" should not divert our attention from the fact that life is a continuing series of organism-environment interactions that rarely conform to neat theoretical models. There are, however, sufficient regularities in the developmental process to justify referring to stages in a person's acquisition of adaptive abilities during the course of his or her life. Such stages represent successive states of equilibrium between a person's ability to regulate, and to be regulated by, the environment. These states of equilibrium are continuously disrupted by changes occurring within the person or within the surrounding environment. Such disruptions prompt people to grow psychologically as they seek ever more inclusive ways of adjusting to their environment. Physiological maturation is one source of growth-producing change in that it alters a person's capacity for agency in the world. The successive acquisition of abilities to crawl, walk, talk, play with peers, read, and understand abstract concepts all reflect the way in which physical maturation naturally leads to new stages of psychological development. Changes in the social environment also elicit sustained psychological change and growth. Intermittent absences from the mother, demands to regulate one's own body functions, schooling, dating, child rearing, struggling with great moral and intellectual problems, and the contemplation of one's own imminent death likewise successively expand the "environment" to which the person must adapt both through agency and through enhanced receptivity or mutuality.

The self thus develops through its interactions with the wider environment. Nurtured in the medium of personal relationships, the self must acquire the skills of agency and mutuality that will insure fulfillment as the "environment" grows ever wider. Perhaps the most helpful tool for organizing our examination of this process is Erik Erikson's delineation of the eight stages of the human life cycle. Grounded in psychoanalytic theory, Erikson's model recognizes the strong role of nonconscious forces such as instincts and other organismic urges in shaping human behavior. Yet, in contrast to classical psychoanalytic thought, Erikson places equal emphasis on the role of the social environment in stimulating us to action. Furthermore, Erikson understands the conscious personality or ego as having the capacity to control and regulate a person's relationships with the environment in ways that, within limits, supersede both genetic/ instinctual tendencies and social conditioning. And, finally, Erikson's theory has strong sociobiological dimensions in that it never takes the perspective of the individual as final but instead insists upon interpreting all personal development in light of its contributions to the sequence of generations as understood ecologically.

Erikson directs our attention to the fact that a person faces "adaptive challenges" much the way that species do in their effort to survive and to extend the range of their satisfaction. Over the course of life we face a series of such challenges that require us to acquire new methods for relating to, and interacting with, our social environments. Erikson refers to these adaptive challenges as "crises" because in each case they represent a collapse of earlier modes of adapting to the environment and engage the person in a struggle to develop new and more sophisticated means of effectively regulating, and being regulated by, the changing vistas of his or her environment. Each stage thus represents an important moment in which older patterns of relating to the world have become too narrow or too idiosyncratic to be of further adaptive use. Continued personal growth requires the learning of new emotional, behavioral, and mental repertoires. Erikson depicts psychological growth as proceeding according to an epigenetic principle whereby new and more highly structured stages emerge from earlier, less differentiated ones. The epigenetic principle highlights the fact that later and more advanced psychological stages build upon, and carry forward, earlier stages (as well as our more fundamental instinctual impulses and tendencies). Without remaining an expression of our most basic biological drives and our earliest psychological nature, later developmental achievements are not truly stronger or adaptive. Full and resilient psychological growth requires an ongoing integration of what is early and late, biological and social, instinctual and rational.

In Erikson's view, it is crucial that enhanced capacity for agency always be balanced by an equally enhanced capacity for mutuality. Because he takes the life cycle in its entirety as his framework for understanding personal development, Erikson is quick to point out that every life is interlocked with others at each stage of its change and growth. Beginning with conception, there is no such thing as a self-made person—individuals are not islands unto themselves. Like cogwheels that move forward by meshing or interconnecting with other cogwheels, we require the presence and actions of others at every stage of development. The interdependence of people in the cogwheeling of generations (what sociobiologists would refer to as the transmission of genes) ensures a mutuality between each person and his or her social world. Erikson refers to this necessary interdependence as *mutual activation*. By this he means that we grow in the very act of helping others to grow. The structure of the life cycle is such that at each major stage growth occurs through—and only through—activity that extends us out to others. The evolution of the human species has been such as to insure a certain complementarity between the needs of the young and old. For example, a mother tirelessly gives of herself to her young child without any consideration of her own needs; but paradoxically, in the process she becomes fulfilled as a woman and mother. The same would be true of two friends or two persons in love. Only when you finally escape self-centeredness and truly care for another will you ever activate real love in yourself. You grow and fulfill yourself as you help others grow and become fulfilled. In Erikson's words, human growth "depends from stage to stage upon a network of mutual influences" within which people actuate others even as they are actuated, and within which "the person is inspired with active properties" even as each person inspires others.[6] To this extent Erikson helps us to locate care at the very crux of the developmental process. Care directs the skills of agency or effective action in ways that enhance, rather than dissolve, mutuality. It actuates growth or fulfillment in the self even as it establishes the self in a wider and more nurturant "network of mutual influences."

Childhood and the Beginning of Agency

The self only gradually emerges from its initial condition of embeddedness. The fetus has no identity distinct from its uterine environment and, upon birth, is thrust into the world wholly lacking a sense of individuality or self-directed agency. The newborn seems to have no identity separate from the nurturing parent. The infant's sense of security, as well as his or her rudimentary sense of self, is "mirrored" to it from this parent. The parent possesses a grandeur that is idealized by the infant, and he or she gains a sense of being prized and important by virtue of being connected with this idealized image of the parent. According to psychoanalytically oriented theorists such as Melanie Klein, Otto Kernberg, D. W. Winnicott, and Heinz Kohut, the principal challenge of the first two years of life—a challenge that will continue throughout life—is that of gradually separating our own self-image from the image of the nurturing parent (or the various persons, ideals, or religious beliefs that assume the role of "idealized object" later in life). Beginning with these earliest encounters with a loving parent, humans are caught between the two compelling and conflicting psychological needs that we described above. On the one hand, we are driven by the need to have a prized, cohesive sense of self; we have the need to stand out, be separate, and express ourselves through effective action that furthers our own interests in the world. On the other hand, we have an equally compelling need for merger or communion with a larger whole or an idealized image (such as the perfect parent or, in late life, with some image of God) from which we will receive security and, via our attachment to that valued object, receive a sense of meaningfulness.

What is important for us to underscore is that beginning in infancy, and extending throughout life, healthy and effective selfhood depends upon this ability to feel intimately united with valued persons or some "higher reality" from which the self receives both its sense of intrinsic worth and of being intrinsically related to the world. The failure of such a psychological sense of relationship thwarts the optimal development of a mature sense of self and fates people to a pathological narcissism in which they are utterly dominated by the need to find external signs of their self-worth. People who lack a felt-sense of intrinsic worth and intimate relationship to the world generally create protective barriers to prevent further emotional harm, become exceptionally manipulative in relationships, and are almost incapable of feeling or caring for others in their own right. Under optimal conditions, however, our original relatedness to an idealized "other" (the nurturing parent) is gradually replaced by other warm and reciprocal relationships that will make it possible for us to extend into life without unnecessary defenses and to recognize the needs and worth of others. Put differently, the kinds of "mutuality" that we acquire throughout the course of development determine the degree to which we will be able to live the life of moral caring as adults. They will determine whether we can approach life with minimal distortion and perceive the awe and wonder embodied in the living beings about us. When our defenses are in abeyance and distortion is at a minimum, life lures us out to meet it and to care for it as acts of intrinsic merit. Our capacity for moral relatedness as we progress through life thus depends upon the extent to which we acquire personality strengths that will permit full and undistorted relatedness to others.

The need to find an optimal balance between agency and mutuality commences with infancy. The first step toward this goal begins with what Erik Erikson describes as the challenge of securing a basic trust in life. By this Erikson means that the critical theme in the first year of life concerns whether the child experiences life as something that can and should be trusted rather than feared as a chaotic, hostile thing. The degree to which infants are able to trust the world depends mostly on the quality of care they receive from the mother. The infant whose needs are met promptly, whose discomforts are quickly removed, who is cuddled, fondled, played with, and talked to, develops a sense that the world is a safe place to be and that people are dependable and helpful. If, on the other hand, the care is inconsistent and inadequate, the infant never develops a truly trusting and positive attitude toward the world and other people. To this extent, the resolution of this first and important developmental challenge is in most respects outside a person's arena of influence. His or her psychological strength is dependent upon the quality of care provided by the people from the previous generation to whom this child came as a responsibility—whether by choice or by accident. A good culture nurtures its members and, through its methods of socialization, imparts to its young the trust that will permit them to venture forth into life "knowing" that their basic wishes can be obtained in spite of the many obstacles that will confront them from time to time.

As infants gain trust in their mother and world, they start to discover their own capacity to act and cause effects in their environment. Between the ages of two and four they begin to assert a degree of autonomy; they begin to realize their capacity to desire or will. The second task of psychological development, then, is that of acquiring a sense of autonomy while combatting shame and doubt. The crisis that defines this stage is occasioned by the child's opposing desires to maintain dependence upon the parents and to exercise this growing autonomy. The kind and quality of parental care exerted during this stage imparts lasting direction upon the child's psychological development. Parents must help their children balance self-initiated actions with the restraints imposed upon them by society. Parents must be careful to encourage active play and experimentation while simultaneously putting a limit on their actions so that they will not hurt themselves or become utterly undisciplined. Punishment begins in this stage and, when administered with insight into the process of psychological development, this punishment is a fundamental part of parental care. Punishment is necessary for placing helpful limitations on the child's growing autonomy, but it can all too easily cause doubt and shame which will cripple any further development of autonomy. The type of behavior parents permit and the way in which they exert control over the child will have a direct bearing upon his or her attitude toward ideals, authority, and social organizations later in life. The point here is that the type of parenting a child receives in this stage determines his or her attitudes toward authority—how much authority does he or she have as an individual and how much does society have? Are individual actions valuable or are they going to be punished? Ideally children acquire in this stage strength of will, the capacity to exercise free choice as well as self-restraint, in spite of unavoidable moments of shame and doubt. Again, it must be emphasized that the growing child's capacity for agency and will is mediated by the quality of care provided by her or his parents and social environment.

By the fourth or fifth year a child has matured enough to express the urge to live in an exuberant, unharnessed way. During the third stage of development the child must acquire a sense of initiative that will carry this urge forward while overcoming the sense of guilt that inevitably accompanies those actions deemed wrong by authorities. Whether children emerge from this stage with a healthy sense of initiative depends largely upon how parents respond to their self-initiated activities. Children who are given much freedom and opportunity to initiate motor play such as running, wrestling, sports, or general play around the home will have their sense of initiative reinforced. Initiative is also reinforced when parents answer their children's questions (intellectual initiative). Conversely, if children are made to feel that their actions are upsetting to the parent or that their questions are a nuisance then they will invariably feel uneasy and even guilty about their own desires and actions. Such guilt may well persist through later life stages, leaving the person without a sense of confidence or assertiveness. With responsible parenting children in this stage of development develop a sense of purpose and initiative that permits them to envisage and pursue goals without being inhibited by fear of punishment or guilt.

Between the ages of six and eleven children begin to participate in ever-widening social environments. This is the point at which the environment expands to include others of their own age. Children's energies now become harnessed to social adjustment and mastering the rules that govern friendship. During these years a child enters the fourth stage of personality development, in which he or she must master the tasks of self-improvement and of learning to perform tasks skillfully and to interact successfully with other people. The child's drive to succeed now includes an awareness of the possibility of failure. This underlying fear impels young children to work harder to succeed and to ward off feelings of mediocrity. It is crucial that the child not develop a sense of inferiority, so that the child will possess the self-assurance to move confidently forward in life. During this stage children must acquire a sense of industry while fending off perceptions of personal inferiority. The successful resolution of the challenges imposed upon the child during these years requires the sense of personal competency in actively using both intelligence and physical skills to complete tasks, unimpaired by feelings of inferiority.

The predominant developmental themes throughout these first four stages of the life cycle concern the need for enhancing one's skills at agency. The changes resulting from physical maturation and from an expanding social environment require children to develop ever-increasing effectiveness in expressing their individuality. The fact that those developmental themes related to agency are at the forefront during these years should not, however, divert our attention from the developing child's sense of belonging to a greater whole (parental and ontological). The emerging personality is fashioned out of the ingredients provided by the nurturing environment. And, for this reason, the child's sense of relatedness to others continues to provide the medium of psychological growth. For example, most of a developing child's skills and attitudes are learned through *imitation* and *identification*. Children begin imitating their parents and older siblings at a very early age. Play, speech, waving bye-bye, and eating behaviors all begin through attempts at imitation. Trust, autonomy, initiative, and industry are likewise passed from one generation to another through the role models that parents and other significant adults provide. The other major avenue of early socialization is the process whereby children learn to identify with significant people in their environment. Identification with parents or older siblings hastens a child's acquisition of attitudes and behaviors that will enable him or her to adjust to the larger social world. Importantly, however, both imitation and identification are vehicles of learning that operate only along the pathways opened up by the degree and quality of "mutuality" adhering between the child and those upon whom she or he is dependent. When basic trust pervades the person's orientation to the world, barriers can be let down and genuine reciprocity enhances the learning process. An uncaring environment offers no medium of wider identification and closes off the child's capacity to acknowledge or appreciate life in ways that go beyond issues of immediate self-defense.

Adolescence and Early Adulthood: The Formation and Extension of Identity

The teenage years witness the full development of a person's capacity for agency. The body develops in strength and stamina until physical maturation is reached and the child is transformed into a young man or young woman. During this stage of life our cognitive skills also mature and we become able to engage in higher-level, abstract thought for the first time in our lives. The noted cognitive psychologist Jean Piaget demonstrated that thinking skills develop through a series of successive stages. Beginning with the simplest reflex or sensorimotor behaviors in infants, mental skills develop gradually as the individual learns to incorporate ever-widening ranges of life into his or her repertoire of adaptive behaviors. By the teenage years, the capacity for abstract thought makes it possible for a person to construct mental or hypothetical responses to any given situation and imagine the likely consequences of these responses before acting. At this stage in life it becomes possible to imagine acting in a variety of ways, of being a wide variety of persons.

It is precisely this capacity for abstract and hypothetical reasoning that makes the issue of "identity" so acute during adolescence and early adulthood. Questions such as, Who am I? Who should I become? and What do I believe in? no longer have simple answers. Each can now be approached from any number of angles; numerous possibilities can be entertained. What is more, the moral and religious beliefs acquired earlier in life that might help guide persons through these perplexing questions no longer carry with them an automatic authority. Young adults begin to detect relativity in ideas formerly assumed to be absolute, hypocrisy amidst what before was thought to be utter sincerity, logical contradictions among what were earlier thought to be compatible methods for ascertaining what is true, right, or good.

It is amidst this intellectual bewilderment that young adults must acquire a sense of identity and overcome the potential confusion that threatens to make the establishment of a firm personal identity impossible. This, the fifth of Erikson's eight stages, signals the fact that the developing person is at a pivotal period in the life cycle and is shifting from the status of being dependent upon adults to becoming an adult. Erikson has pointed out that one of the most important dimensions of identity formation is that of acquiring a unified set of beliefs or a philosophy of life capable of giving a convincing set of guidelines, rules, and principles for action. Erikson uses the word "ideology" to refer to the "system of commanding ideas" that enables an individual to take a firm hold upon life and make confident decisions in the face of seeming ambiguity. Ideologies afford young people a cognitive tool with which to get a handle on life and to solidify their identity. They make it possible for young people to understand their place in the greater scheme of things by providing a comprehensive explanation of how life operates and how people should chart their course through life.

The ideologies people internalize—be they formulated from formal religious traditions, "how to succeed" philosophies found in popular culture, or random images of the "good life" arbitrarily selected from personal experience—have long-lasting consequences for the subsequent development of personal growth. They tell us what we should value, who we should want to be with, and how we should want to be with them. In short, they will guide what we will decide to care for and how we will go about translating that care into action. Full agency, then, requires an intellectual "map" that guides us to effective action in the world. Unfortunately, our society gives precious little attention to whether the maps or ideologies it provides are also capable of guiding people to enhanced mutuality in their relationships to self, to others, and to the natural environment.

Personal identity is, in the final analysis, never solely "personal." We are created every bit as much from the nutrients of our social ecosystem as plants are emergent creations of their biological ecosystems. Our identities are meted out in the give and take of interpersonal relationships; they are received as well as achieved. And, if the larger network of social life is to remain healthy and viable, we must actively give back the same kind of nurturant strength we have absorbed in the process of our growth and development. Ideologies that do not direct us to enhance our sense of mutuality with others are thus poorly suited to human fulfillment. The obvious truth of this fundamental principle of the human ecosystem becomes clearer as we reach middle age.

The sixth stage of the life cycle pertains to the experiences of courtship, marriage, and early parenting years. In young adulthood the pendulum typically beings to swing away from preoccupation with the enhancement of personal agency and instead points personal growth in the direction of seeking enhanced forms of relatedness with others. Erikson describes the essential task of this stage as that of acquiring a sense of intimacy while avoiding the possible fate of going through life in relative isolation. Intimacy here means more than physical lovemaking. Erikson is instead referring to the ability to share with, and care about, another person without fear of losing oneself in the process. Intimacy, then, is love without defensiveness and without continual preoccupation with oneself. Those who do not establish the capacity for intimacy with a close friend or marriage partner become increasingly isolated from the social mainstream and soon find themselves with no one to share with, or care for.

The major developmental theme of this period involves psychological readiness for sustained interpersonal commitment. Readiness for intimacy includes the ability, and even more so the desire, to share mutual trust and to regulate periods of work, recreation, and procreation for each partner's fullest satisfaction. This stage of life requires us to enhance our capacity for giving and receiving love. Love here refers to the reestablishment of mutuality as over and against agency as the dominant mode with which one engages in close personal relationships. Those possessing firm identities are capable of a mutuality in which it is possible to establish a "way of life" that binds two separate persons together in a mutually enhancing manner.

Middle Adulthood: Mutuality and Generativity

Adulthood brings the reemergence of mutuality as a critical mode of personhood. After many years of focusing upon building skills associated with agency, adulthood presents a series of developmental challenges that reveal that sustained human fulfillment requires a deepened sense of mutuality and of participation in a greater social—and even ontological—whole. By the age of thirty most people have reached the peak of their capacity for agency and productivity in the world. This is the phase of life when people have fully learned how to create. Marriages, children, life-styles, and careers are all created in the transition into adulthood. Yet, the very things that our honed skills at "agency" create eventually lead us to discover the larger conception of the "cycle" of life. Up to this point we have viewed the life cycle as the span of years from birth to death. Yet there is also the sense in which our individual lives are to be understood in terms of the sequence of generations. Each life interconnects with those preceding and following it. In our youth the quality of our personal lives is dependent upon the kind of care we receive from an older generation; in maturity our fulfillment is in large part determined by how we "recycle" our lives in our offspring and their generation. The concept of the life cycle thus introduces us to the "ecology" of human generations. It invokes the idea of an ecosystem in which all the separate living organisms are ultimately interconnected. The human ecosystem, like biological ecosystems, links each of its members together in an organic whole. The actions of each member of the system have long-term consequences in terms of the readiness of the environment to nurture healthy development.

The seventh, and longest, stage of the life cycle is dominated by what Erikson describes as the need to acquire a sense of generativity and to avoid a sense of self-absorption. By generativity Erikson means "primarily the concern in establishing and guiding the next generation."[7] Generativity thus need not entail biological parenting per se. Rather, it has a wider meaning that entails such forms of creativity as "new products and new ideas." Generativity concerns a widening sense of responsibility to care for persons and issues that transcend one's own immediate well-being out of a sense of responsibility for the world which future generations will inhabit. Generativity is thus defined by an active caring for the welfare of others, especially the young, by making the world a better place in which to live. Those who fail to establish a vital sense of generativity typically fall into a state of self-absorption in which their personal needs and comforts remain the predominant concern.

Erikson has drawn attention to the fact that evolution "has made man a teaching as well as a learning animal, for dependence and maturity are reciprocal: mature man *needs to be needed,* and maturity is guided by the nature of that which must be cared for."[8] The human species is the product of a complex interplay between genetic dispositions and cultural forms that either release or impart behaviors which the young need in order to grow and prosper. Generativity, then, is at the core of our evolutionary heritage and can be understood as the predisposition both in animals and in humans to "instinctively encourage in their young what is ready for release."[9] Considered sociobiologically, generativity is "the instinctual power behind various forms of selfless 'caring.' "[10] Cultures that reinforce and help elicit this natural inclination to generativity help to instill in their members the strength or virtue of care. Care, as Erikson observes, "is the widening concern for what has been generated by love, necessity, or accident [and] overcomes the ambivalence adhering to irreversible obligation."[11]

The challenges and tasks associated with midlife generativity accentuate the moral dimensions of responsible human existence. In recent years there has been an outpouring of literature concerning midlife developmental stages.[12] While largely reconfirming Erikson's general scheme, these studies have added a great deal of additional insight into the changing nature of personal fulfillment across the life span. Daniel Levinson's often-cited *Seasons of a Man's Life* is perhaps the most helpful of these accounts of midlife transitions.[13] Although Levinson's study focused on middle-class American males and is thus in need of critical reassessment through the balancing vision of theorists such as Carol Gilligan, it nonetheless helps us to map the major phases of adult development and to understand the growing "need" that humans have for mutuality and generativity in their adult years.[14] Levinson suggests that middle age consists of two distinct eras: early adulthood, which covers the approximate age span of twenty-two to forty, and middle adulthood which begins at about forty and continues to the age of sixty (when one enters late adulthood, which will be examined in the next section). The first era of adulthood begins when a person in his or her twenties enters the world of adult vocational and familial responsibilities. This is a time when initial decisions must be made about one's occupation, love relationships, marriage possibilities, and preferred life-style. Levinson's studies revealed that decisions such as these usually coincide with the formulation of a "dream." This dream typically has to do with vocational and economic success and is defined largely in terms of promotions, income, status, and social influence. Also, the "dream" symbolizes a person's major aspirations and, therefore, values concerning the ideal state of personal fulfillment. It follows that this dream reflects the kind of ideology around which a person's identity has been forged and reveals the great extent to which the materialistic bias of our culture dictates a person's real values, regardless of her or his professed moral or religious beliefs. And, too, this dream is usually chosen according to a person's perceptions of his or her skills and capacities for agency. Seldom, especially in males, does this dream entail any real vision of who we most want to be with or just how we want to be with them.

The transition between early and middle adulthood comes in subtle ways. For the most part, the transition consists of growing awareness of a gradual diminishment in one's bodily vigor combined with periods of doubt and partial dissatisfaction with one's chosen dream. For the first time it is possible to estimate one's social or economic trajectory with reasonable accuracy. Careers are sufficiently established that one's position on the ladder leading to "the top" is evident. Most of us must finally understand that our dream will never be realized in full. As the dream undergoes such an assault it is usually modified and adjusted to more realistic standards of accomplishment. With this change in our personal goals come many perplexing questions: What have I done in my life? Would I choose the same path if I had it to do over again? What do I get from my job, my spouse, my family? What do I give my job, my spouse, my family? In the years that I have left, what do I most want to accomplish and what will "count" for a worthwhile life? In and through these questions we gradually discern that, in the long run, personal fulfillment depends less on external measurements of our capacity for agency than it does on the depth of our mutuality with the wider environments we inhabit.

Most of the "crises" faced in midlife cannot be solved through the kind of instrumental reasoning processes that enable us to set career objectives and master the successive tasks to bring us to that goal. They do not pose the challenge of finding means to a socially defined end but rather with making personal decisions about which ends are truly worth pursuing. For example, Lawrence Kohlberg's studies of adult development reveal that in midlife we become profoundly aware of the irreversibility of our choices and decisions. That is, when we are young we believe that life has limitless possibilities and that if we are not satisfied with earlier choices we can always change our minds and simply strike out in new directions. By midlife we become aware of how earlier decisions and actions shaped our lives in irreversible ways. Put negatively, we are "trapped" in careers, marriages, and life-styles by our own earlier decisions. This awareness adds extra poignancy to the decisions being made in midlife about whether to continue with our present careers, marriages, and life-styles. We are aware that we shape our own destiny through these decisions. In midlife we realize that there really is no world "out there" to which we are seeking to adapt, but rather that we actually create our worlds by the values we hold and how well we are able to bring these values into existence.

The most haunting doubt at this period of life, according to Kohlberg, is that of whether it really "pays" to try to be moral, to care for and try to help others. The sustained care for the welfare of others demanded of us during our parenting years leads to profound questions concerning whether there really is a moral order in life. If it is we who engender an order onto life by the values we hold, then what kind of values should we be teaching the young to respect? And, too, should we bother to stand for any set of moral obligations if it is indeed possible that the universe is either indifferent or perhaps even hostile to such efforts? Even those people who have previously attained a clear awareness of universal ethical principles frequently become skeptical concerning why, in a universe that is largely unjust, we should commit ourselves to a moral rather than a personally hedonistic life-style. Kohlberg observes that in midlife

> the answer to the question "Why be moral?" at this level entails the question "Why live?" (and the parallel question, "How face death?") so that ultimate moral maturity requires a mature solution to the question of the meaning of life. This, in turn, is hardly a moral question per se; it is an ontological or a religious one. Not only is the question not a moral one but it is not a question resolvable on purely logical or rational grounds as moral questions are.[15]

The experience of sustained responsibility for one's own and others' lives thus finally prompts persons to contemplate their place in the greater scheme of things. What is at question here is not one's capacity for effective agency in the physical and economic environments, but one's mutuality in the ultimate sense of relatedness to meanings that can be affirmed as intrinsic to life. We might prefigure some themes that will emerge in the final chapter of this book by noting that Kohlberg compared the state of mind that finally grasps the ultimate reason for caring, the ultimate meaning of living, to what Spinoza called "the union of the mind with the whole frame of nature." Kohlberg's studies of adult development led him to conclude that moral vision is in some ultimate sense related to mystical or contemplative experiences in which the ego is transcended. He wrote, "The logic of such experience is sometimes expressed in theistic terms, but it need not be. Its essential is the sense of being a part of the whole of life and the adoption of a cosmic, as opposed to a [purely humanistic] perspective."[16]

Other midlife challenges also prompt persons to turn their attention away from issues of adapting to socioeconomic structures and instead to those less tangible meanings of life that are not "out there" in any straightforward or obvious way. It takes most of us until middle age to learn how fragile life really is. When young, we assume that mistakes can be overcome, that everyone is strong and resilient, and that "everything will turn out okay." As we get older we have seen too many tragic deaths, too many lives ruined by self-destructive behavior, too many disintegrated marriages, and too many emotionally crushed persons to continue the carefree attitude of youth. The fragility of human life, both physically and emotionally, prompts us to want to put into place as many safeguards as possible to protect ourselves and our young from our own recklessness. The "conservatism" of age is thus in many respects an emerging awareness of the preciousness—and precariousness—of life and the growing desire to care for it by minimizing the risks of damage.

By middle adulthood it also becomes apparent that we cannot accomplish an infinite number of things in a single lifetime. There will always be unfinished tasks, new roads to travel, new possessions to acquire. Thus, what is needed is some kind of perspective from which to sort out and arrange life's many opportunities and experiences into some kind of pattern that will reveal which ones are ultimately worth pursuing. We no longer ask ourselves what *can* I do, but rather what *should* a person do with his or her life? It was precisely this shift from issues of agency in the material world to ones of mutuality in the interpersonal and even cosmic spheres of life that psychologist Carl Jung had in mind when he observed that his patients over thirty-five "all have been people whose problem in the last resort was that of finding a religious outlook on life."[17] What Jung referred to is the fact that nearly every midlife crisis can be reduced to the individual's need for an understanding of how his or her life participates in something that transcends the span of a single human life and can thus be affirmed as having some intrinsic meaning or value.

Late Adulthood: Concern for Life in the Face of Death

The eighth and final developmental challenge that Erikson detects in the human life cycle is that of acquiring a sense of integrity and avoiding despair in old age. As adults begin to finish their work of furnishing tangible support to the next generation, they simultaneously begin to see their lives more clearly in terms of their participation in this sequence of generations. This is a time for reflection, for reminiscing about one's life now viewed as a whole. Experiences are sifted through during daydreams and recollections. The many values that guided our judgments in the past (e.g., gaining prestige, wealth, or power) have lost their relevancy. Our actions are consequently viewed not for how fully they served as effective means to socially defined ends, but for how they might now be understood as ends in themselves. For this reason, psychological health becomes less dependent upon skills that adapt us to the material and economic environments. Instead, our self-worth becomes increasingly tied up with our ability to affirm that our lives contributed something of meaning and enduring value to the sequence of generations.

Integrity accrues to those who can look back on their lives with satisfaction. For many, of course, extended reminiscences point out only the missed opportunities and thus lead to an overriding sense of despair. The successful resolution of these inevitable threats to self-worth requires the attainment of a wider perspective in which we can affirm something of enduring value in our lives. In this sense old age and the approach of death complete the life cycle by bringing us back to a developmental crisis similar to that of infancy. Acquiring integrity, as with acquiring basic trust, depends upon a sense of fundamental connectedness with something of an "ontologically higher or more ultimate" nature. What the mother is for the infant, the ongoing chain of human generations is to the individual confronting death. Integrity, as with basic trust, comes from a mode of mutuality that cuts deeper than the subject-object relationship of everyday adult experience. As Erikson observed,

> Every human being's Integrity may be said to be religious (whether explicitly or not). Each person engages in an inner search for, and a wish to communicate with, that mysterious, that Ultimate Other: for there can be no "I" without an "Other" and no "We" without a shared "Other".[18]

Implicit in Erikson's remark is the suggestion that when confronted with the adaptive challenges of old age, we seek out the "shared 'Other' " that underlies and connects our individual lives. It is this shared Other that bestows an intrinsic meaning upon the various things we have done to affirm the human "others" we have engaged along life's path. It is perhaps also implicit in Erikson's remark that the only certain way of reaching out to God—to the shared Other—is to care actively and meaningfully for the lives with which we have become interconnected, whether by chance or by deliberate decision.

Integrity, like trust, is an inward disposition that is irreducible to judgments about this or that feature of life, but instead pertains to the intrinsic goodness of life in spite of inevitable instances of pain or loss. We cannot find integrity in our own life unless we can affirm that life itself possesses a fundamental or intrinsic integrity that does not diminish or perish with our own physical death. It is with this in mind that Erikson believes that the search for integrity makes possible human virtue or strength of wisdom. At one level, wisdom represents a growing clarity in our identification of what things are truly worth valuing and pursuing. At another level, wisdom reflects the affirmation of values conducive to strengthening life even in the face of death. Such a psychological achievement makes it possible to affirm the miraculous and sacred quality of life over and against any perspective that would instead focus principally on tragedy and pain. Wisdom affirms that what is actualized in life has meaning or value principally insofar as it expresses something that is intrinsic to life. In religious terms this means that life is to be evaluated by how fully it expresses the creative intentions of the First Cause, or God. Wisdom is thus the attainment of a perspective that refuses to grant final or ultimate status to humanity's concerns with social and economic standards of importance. Instead, wisdom is more concerned with something more cosmological and ontological; it cares for those forms of life that "count for something" even after our bodies and worldly treasures have dissipated.

Much of the "death and dying literature" written in the past twenty years has similarly focused upon the individual's need for the ability to understand just how his or her life has participated in something that transcends the individual life span. Elisabeth Kübler-Ross's well-known *On Death and Dying,* for example, maintains that humans psychologically adapt to the inevitability of their own death by going through the successive phases of denial, anger, bargaining, depression, and finally acceptance.[19] For Kübler-Ross, a mature and healthy acceptance of one's own imminent death can be achieved in one of two principal ways. The first path to acceptance of our finitude might be called the "horizontal" path in that it has to do with finding integrity in one's completed life tasks. She found that patients who can look back over their lives and confidently affirm that they have contributed to the well-being of others find consolation and meaning even in death. They know that they have contributed to the sequence of generations and thereby rest content with the dignity of having given back to life all that they have taken from it. A tangible part of their lives will live on in those whom they have affirmed and strengthened.

Kübler-Ross also found that those rare individuals who possess what she called an "intrinsic religious faith" readily find acceptance of death. That is, in contrast to the essentially humanistic path that affirms integrity in terms of our concrete actions toward other persons, this is the "vertical" path that affirms integrity in terms of our participation in an order of life that quite literally transcends the physical world. Her interviews with dying patients revealed that some persons find the wisdom to accept death long before they approach serious illness. Having developed a spiritual vision of life, they had long ago come to identify themselves not as a body who possibly possesses a soul, but rather as a soul who possesses a body. Their ability to identify themselves as inhabiting a spiritual environment (over and beyond the natural and social environments) opened up for them a way of looking at the world in which their caring acts could be affirmed as participating in something of infinite, rather than finite, value.

The Ontogenetic Groundplan of Care

In the first chapter we introduced the concept of ecology as a means of understanding human behavior in its most inclusive contexts. An ecological perspective teaches us that parts are constitutive of wholes, and that the meanings of parts are determined relationally by their participation in the whole.[20] This principle would also seem to hold for the social ecosystem within which psychological development unfolds. Developmental psychology furnishes empirical descriptions of the "average expectable" crises or challenges that call for ever new and more comprehensive adaptive strategies. It would also seem to be established empirically that there is something along the order of an ontogenetic groundplan that leads persons gradually to moral commitment. Forging intimate relationships, sustaining responsibility for the welfare of the young, recognizing the frailty and finitude of personal life, and anticipating one's own imminent death all successively widen our conceptions of the environment in which we live and have our being.

Seen in developmental perspective, the capacity for moral caring is an emergent property within the human ecosystem. Individuals are not born with the ability to assume a moral perspective on life. Nor, in fact, do many persons ever attain the ability for principled moral thought. Yet, as the developmental studies of Kohlberg have shown, moral thought can be distinguished from simple conformity with socially sanctioned rules and can be shown to be a psychological achievement that emerges only through successful adaptations to predictable challenges confronted throughout the life cycle.[21] Kohlberg has detected six distinct stages of cognitive organization in the development of our moral thinking. These stages represent a sequential transition from the largely egocentric ethical orientation during early childhood to a fully principled level of moral thought characterized by justice and universality, which emerges, if ever, during adulthood.

Kohlberg's studies of moral development confirm Erikson's contention that the capacity for true generativity is a relatively late ontogenetic development and emerges from those life experiences that prompt (1) a personal acceptance of the ideal adequacy of certain principles of conduct and (2) a personal willingness to commit oneself and act upon these principles for their own sake even though there may be no direct economic or material reward for doing so. Sustained responsibility for the welfare of others prompts us to look for those principles of action that would seem best suited to providing care in a comprehensive or inclusive way. Kohlberg has, furthermore, shown that those individuals who acquire this inclusive mode of caring utilize a form of moral reasoning that has distinct cognitive properties. He contends that individuals who have attained "fully-principled" moral thought display logical comprehensiveness, universality, and consistency in their thinking about the principles of effective care. Their reasoning conforms not to contractual obligations or positivistic analyses of rights, but rather to an appeal to those ingredients or properties thought to be indispensable to an ideal human community, even though such a community has never been empirically actualized. Kohlberg attempted to summarize the formal characteristics of fully developed moral thought in his observation that "personally chosen moral principles are also principles of justice, the principles any member of society would choose for that society if he did not know what his position was to be in the society and in which he might be the least advantaged."[22] In other words, Kohlberg believes that fully principled moral thought entails the formal cognitive properties of reversibility and mutuality.

There may well be some inherent flaws in Kohlberg's research methods and particularly with his forced construction of stages that progressively approximate Kant's categorical imperative and John Rawls's theory of morality as justice. Nonetheless it would seem that he has demonstrated fairly conclusively that moral rationality is neither the operation of an inborn faculty for intuiting transcendental truths nor a passive reflection of facts found in the natural environment. Moral thought, it would seem, is instead the gradually more inclusive form of decision making motivated by those life circumstances that encourage nonegoistic commitment to an ideal community of care.[23]

There is, then, an ontogenetic groundplan that locates care in our gradual transition into situations in which we are entrusted with nurturing others. In these moments, personal fulfillment depends as much on giving as it does on receiving satisfaction. The irony of care is that while it is an attempt to use our capacities for agency on behalf of others, it nonetheless contributes to our psychological fulfillment by occasioning personal growth. It was with this in mind that Erikson suggested that developmental psychology sheds new light on the relationships of agency and mutuality and could thus provide a reformulated version of the Golden Rule:

> Truly worthwhile acts enhance a mutuality between the doer and the other—a mutuality which strengthens the doer even as it strengthens the other. Thus, the "doer" and "the other" are partners in one deed.

Seen in the light of human development, this means that the doer is
activated in whatever strength is appropriate to his age, stage, and
condition, even as he activates in the other the strength appropriate
to his age, stage, and condition. Understood this way, the Rule would
say that it is best to do to another what will strengthen you even as it
will strengthen him—that is, what will develop his best potential even
as it develops your own.[24]

Developmental psychology thus supplies another perspective on our
question, Who cares? Considered psychologically, care is not simply a
subjective sentiment. It is a developmental achievement that depends, in
part, upon a favorable environment in which proper parenting and
prevailing ideologies elicit and strengthen the growing capacity for
genuine reciprocity in interpersonal relationships. The capacity to care
requires the acquisition of personality strengths (e.g., autonomy, will,
initiative) that make possible effective action in the world. It also, and
perhaps more importantly, requires the ability for mutuality and for
regarding others in their own right. The person who cares is the one who
responds to the developmental challenges of finding a deeper mutuality
with others in friendship, love, and parenting. He or she who cares is
someone who has realized that, at least from young adulthood on, human
fulfillment depends as much on giving as it does on receiving satisfaction.
Caring individuals are those who seek assurance that their lives will have
a meaning that transcends the span of their physical existence. They
respond to the challenge to step forward and become stewards of the
sequence of generations. As Erikson put it, "Whatever chance man may
have to transcend the limitations of his ego seems to depend on his prior
ability, in his one and only life cycle, to be fully engaged in the sequence of
generations."[25]

3

Philosophy and the

Ethics of Care

✳

UP TO THIS POINT we have been concerned with the anthropological foundations of care. Care, as we saw in chapter 1, is rooted in our evolutionary-adaptive heritage. Humanity's instinctual activities and innate response tendencies are so phylogenetically constructed as to need to be complemented by cultural tradition. The process of natural selection peculiar to humans operates primarily on our learned or acquired behaviors rather than on our genetic makeup. Among those behaviors that have been "selected for" is the capacity for altruistic or caring action through which we might cooperate for purposes of defense against predators, raise our young to maturity, and form social units in which the division of labor contributes to the population's overall fitness for survival. We are thus genetically fated to be "ethicizing beings." That is, the capacity to care only for self, or even for a small group of kin, would not have been sufficient to promote the survival of the human species. Instead, natural selection favored the capacity for a more generalized caring in which humans might structure their community around a formalized set of rules, duties, and responsibilities. What we think of as advanced ethical theories are not something that emerged out of nothing. Ethical theories are instead "simply an increasingly disinterested and abstracted generalization of the primitive caring that insured the survival of human beings."[1]

Our overview of the course of psychological development likewise shed light on the anthropological foundations of care. Indeed, there would appear to be an ontogenetic groundplan whereby human beings successively acquire the skills for such "generalized caring" and thereby forge a vital, active link in the sequence of generations. Any number of developmental "tasks" prompt us to widen our concern for life: forging intimate relationships, providing the young the same supportive environment that we would have ideally liked to have had ourselves, seeking ways to make our life "count" for something, and pondering over the meaning of existence in the face of our own finitude. Thus a psychological perspective, as with an evolutionary-adaptive perspective, reveals a gradual process whereby an ethical outlook develops in human experience. Rather than being the creation of speculative reason, ethical theories are something more along the lines of "mutations" or "free variations," whereby individual organisms seek to master life's adaptive challenges.

The next step in our investigation of care is to examine more fully what we mean by "generalized caring." We must move from evolutionary-adaptive and psychological perspectives to that of philosophical description and analysis. This shift in perspectives entails the transition from empirical observations to normative judgments. In this chapter we must become clearer about the precise meaning of the word "care" and about whether we can meaningfully discuss or debate our opinions about what makes an action "caring." In short, we must engage in philosophical ethics.

The Crisis of Moral Justification

The philosophical study of ethics is traditionally broken into two distinct fields. The first is referred to as normative ethics and has to do with deriving rules or principles that govern the selection of moral actions. Normative ethical theories generally belong to one of two basic types. The first type of normative theory focuses on the consequences of an action and evaluates moral action in terms of how much happiness, pleasure, well-being, or utility that action produces. This kind of ethical theory, known either as utilitarian or consequentialist ethics, can be further subdivided according to whether the particular theorist emphasizes the utility produced by the specific act or the rule that would ordinarily cover the range of acts to which it belongs. In either case, however, this first type of normative ethics judges an action to be moral according to its consequences or the amount of utility it yields.

The second type of normative ethical theory is usually referred to as formalistic or deontological. Formalistic or deontological theories of ethics do not focus upon the consequences of an action, but rather on the formal properties it embodies. These theories identify the constitutive elements of moral behaviors by looking at the social context in which moral judgments arise and defining the kinds of principles that would define ethical relationships between people. Thus, for example, a deontological ethical theory might specify truth telling or promise keeping as formal elements of moral behavior regardless of the consequences they produce in any given situation. Immanuel Kant's philosophical counterpart to the Golden Rule, known as the categorical imperative, is perhaps the most widely accepted formalist or deontological principle. His imperative that we should "act only on that maxim which [we] can at the same time will to be a universal law" contains within it the recognition that moral behavior is behavior that we are willing to generalize about, that takes the viewpoints of others into consideration, and that incorporates the principle of justice or impartiality (i.e., a principle that would apply equally whether one were initiating an action or the recipient of it). This element of justice has been a prominent concern of formalist theories of ethics in recent years. For example, it is possible to define moral action in a formal way by describing it in terms of that action that would seem just or fair to an "ideal observer" who would view our action in an entirely objective, disinterested way. In one version of the "morality as justice" position, John Rawls suggests that we can begin to discern the formal properties of moral thought simply by imagining that we have the opportunity to choose the rules by which our society will operate but that we do not know in advance what position in this society we will have. Rawls believes that anyone who engages in such an exercise will begin to appreciate why such concepts as impartiality, justice, and fairness constitute formal properties of moral behavior.

The second broad area of ethics is known as metaethics. Metaethics concerns the nature, use, and justification of ethical language. We need to know, for example, what is meant by words such as right, wrong, obligation, responsibility, or virtue. Metaethics has to do with determining whether moral judgments convey knowledge and, if so, what kind of knowledge. Positions on this issue of whether ethical judgments convey knowledge can be classified as belonging to one of two broad types: cognitivist and noncognitivist. Cognitivists assert that moral judgments convey knowledge and are therefore potentially capable of being shown to be true or false. There are several different, and largely incompatible, kinds of cognitivist positions. For example, one form of cognitivism is that of conservative theology. Theological ethics, whether Hindu, Muslim, Jewish, or Christian, claims that ethics are derived from the divine revelations recorded in scripture. Because "true" ethics are based on the scriptural account of God's will, it is possible to make judgments about the truth or falsity of moral judgments. A second type of moral cognitivism is called intuitionism and asserts that moral judgments are intuited by reason much in the same way that valid mathematical principles become rationally self-evident to the alert mind. Intuitionism is sometimes referred to as nonnaturalism in that this view believes that moral principles are not empirically found in nature itself but rather are derived from propositions about humans and their world. Impartiality and justice are examples of principles that some moral philosophers believe are intuitively self-evident to anyone who reflects on the nature of ideal human relationships. A third kind of moral cognitivism is known as naturalism and, unlike intuitionism, contends that moral judgments can be translated into things or events in the natural world and can thus be empirically evaluated.

Noncognitivist positions in the field of metaethics maintain that moral judgments are not statements about facts per se and hence cannot be considered as claims concerning knowledge or truth. One such noncognitivist theory known as emotivism takes the fairly strong position that moral statements reflect nothing more nor less than the speaker's personal preferences. Hence moral judgments such as "It is wrong to lie" are in fact expressions of a person's attitude that "I do not like lying" or else an attempt to express the behavior-shaping mandate "Don't lie." In other words, emotivism contends that moral judgments are subjective, and not verifiable. Other noncognitivist positions (such as the one I will take below) are a bit softer in their insistence that ethical statements do not consist entirely of verifiable factual knowledge. Such views maintain that although moral statements do not contain knowledge in the normal sense, that it is at least possible to assess which moral claims are more reasonable than others and attempt to derive criteria by which the merits of moral judgments can be evaluated.

The modern intellectual climate has favored noncognitivist views of moral discourse. Cognitivist theories of ethics have come under assault from a number of directions, especially from the implications of research in the natural and social sciences. Intuitionists, for example, have failed to specify just what cognitive faculty humans possess that enables them to perceive nonempirical, nonnatural propositions. The methods of psychological science can find no evidence for the existence of a faculty in the brain for intuiting principles that are themselves independent of any and all sense experience. In short, intuitionism lacks intellectual authority because its essential claim concerning the "intuitive" truth of certain ideas lacks any independent confirmation. Theological forms of moral cognitivism run into a similar difficulty when trying to account for the legitimacy of alleged revelations. That is, there is no evidence that can support an individual's claim that he or she has inwardly received divine revelation. And, too, both intuitionists and religious absolutists run into the difficulties posed by the cultural relativism empirically established by our social sciences. That is, the fact that Hindus maintain one set of universal moral truths, Muslims another, and Christians yet another erodes confidence in their claims to revealed knowledge. Similarly, the great variety of "intuited" moral principles finally casts suspicion on their claim to represent universal principles of moral conduct. Of course, the fact of moral relativism does not logically prove that a particular set of moral principles cannot possibly be true, but it does create an intellectual climate that undermines certainty in moral and religious matters.

The attempt of naturalism to establish a factual basis for moral discourse has also been largely unsuccessful. Philosopher G. E. Moore laid the foundations of modern metaethics with his attack on efforts to identify the "good" or the "moral" in terms of some empirically derived understanding of what makes us happy, healthy, and so on. Moore's argument, which in actuality was stated earlier and more clearly in David Hume's writings, points out the logical error involved in committing what he termed "the naturalistic fallacy." The fallacy here has to do with the failure to recognize the different order of thinking entailed in empirical and normative statements. Any statement offering an account of what "is" cannot in itself support an inference about what "ought" to be or "should" be the case. For example, it is one thing to know on the basis of solid empirical evidence that many species of primates engage in homosexual activity. It is quite another thing, however, to know whether homosexual activity can be considered "good," let alone whether we have a moral obligation to do so. Principles of "goodness" and "oughtness" are not themselves present in empirical facts, at least not in any simple or straightforward way. According to the "naturalist fallacy," statements of natural fact do not convey principles of obligation and therefore cannot provide ethics with a factual base.

In sum, there is a crisis in contemporary intellectual thought concerning the issue of moral justification. The consequence of this crisis is that in a time when carelessness is so pervasive in our world, there is no single approach to moral justification that might help sustain and illuminate our efforts to care responsibly for ourselves, our fellow human beings, and the wider ecosystem of which we are a part.

Moral Thought in the Life of Practical Reason

It is against this crisis in moral justification that our investigation of human care becomes especially poignant. We have already begun to lay the foundations of a model of human nature capable of giving clear definition to an ethics of human care. The term *philosophical anthropology* is often used to refer to the attempt to build a model of human experience that is sufficiently comprehensive and generalized so as to define human experience in its many and varied expressions. The "anthropological" dimension of such a model requires a firm basis in natural and social scientific accounts of human nature. The "philosophical" dimension refers to the necessity of integrating into this model a maximally wide range of human experiences, including our moral and religious experiences. Earlier discussions of the emergence and function of care in both the phylogenetic (evolution of the human race) and ontogenetic (evolution of the individual person) development provide the beginning of such an anthropological understanding of care. It also points us in the direction that will enable philosophical understanding and analysis of the ethics of human care.

It is important to situate a discussion of ethics on a larger anthropological model because it is otherwise all too possible to operate according to unrealistic conceptions of the nature and limits of human rationality. Most ethical discussions view the human mind in a naive, pre-Darwinian manner, as though it is essentially some disembodied entity that finds itself amidst the ambiguities of finite existence almost by accident. It is in this context that the philosophical tradition of American pragmatism has so much to offer our present crisis of moral justification. American pragmatism, particularly the formulation given it by psychologist and philosopher William James, clearly understands rationality in terms of its evolutionary-adaptive origins and functions. For example, William James envisioned the mind as a "reflex arc" with three separate, but interrelated parts: (1) the mechanisms that receive sensory impressions, (2) the "central processing" mechanisms that coordinate and structure these impressions in order to formulate an appropriate response, and (3) those mechanisms that facilitate the outgoing discharge or action.[2] The actual term "reflex arc" is somewhat unfortunate in that it perhaps implies that human consciousness is more passive and "merely" reflexive than James actually intended. James's vision of human nature is, after all, the most eloquent defense of humanity's volitional, undetermined, and creative potentials ever to emerge in American psychology. But the term "reflex arc" does help us to appreciate what James meant when he suggested that the fundamental error of philosophy was to attempt to understand the "purely theoretic" elements of rationality as opposed to understanding "rationality in its practical aspect."[3]

Considered in its larger anthropological context, the function of rationality in the human being is to coordinate the central nervous system's adaptive efforts. Considered as an adaptive function, reason is a process rather than a static intellectual faculty. Reason is the activity whereby the world is internally apprehended in ways that make it actable. The function of reason is to render the world amenable to the fulfillment of our various needs and interests. In contrast to those who understand the mind as possessing some faculty for intuiting transcendental principles, James reminds us of the evolutionary-adaptive fact that "the middle stage of consideration or contemplation or thinking is only a place of transit, the bottom of a loop, both whose ends have their point of application in the outer world."[4] We are often deluded into attributing more theoretical power to this "middle stage" of our nervous system's structure than is warranted. As James noted, "sometimes we think it final, and sometimes we fail to see, amid the monstrous diversity in the length and complication of the cogitations which may fill it, that it can have but one essential function and that is the one we have pointed out—the function of defining the direction which our activity shall take."[5]

The concept of practical rationality thus draws our attention to the fact that conceptualization is first, foremost, and always a function within the organism's larger quest to survive and to fulfill a maximum range of its needs and interests. "The cognitive faculty, where it appears to exist at all, appears as but one element in an organic mental whole, and as a minister to higher mental powers,—the powers of will. . . . In plainer English, perception and thinking are only there for behavior's sake."[6] This is not to suggest that the conceptualizing activities of the mind are merely reactive, merely reflexive. On the contrary. The chief difference between humans and other animals lies in the size and capacities of our cerebral cortex. Humans' capacity for abstract and hypothetical representations of the world makes it possible for the human brain not only to conceptualize the world but to transform it as well. That is, our ability for abstract and hypothetical thought makes possible any number of "brain-born" perceptions that re-create reality in ways that—at least potentially—might better serve our rich array of physical, aesthetic, and intellectual needs. The mind can bring creative approaches or proposed solutions to any situation in which newly emerging needs have disrupted the previous equilibrium between us and our environment. These brain-born hypotheses are thus the psychological counterpart of free variations or mutations, which we then introduce into the environment through our action. While most will undoubtedly prove not to be reinforcing, others will achieve for us a higher range of satisfaction and will be "selected for," as it were. Moral thought, we will see, emerges precisely as such "brain-born hypotheses" through which practical reason seeks generalized principles of care.

Obligation, Good, and the Moral Good

We are now in a position to locate the ethics of human care within the life and activity of practical reason. Metaethical questions concerning the definitions of terms such as "good" or "obligation" can be clarified in reference to the activities of practical reason in its efforts to care for life.

The "good" can be understood as whatever contributes to an organism's capacity to embody what the philosopher Alfred North Whitehead described as the threefold urge of beings to live, to live well, and to acquire an increase in satisfaction.[7] In this view the good is not an a priori characteristic of a situation that must be intuited in some transcendental mode of reflection. Rather, the "good" is whatever leads to the satisfaction of the needs and claims of actual organisms in their urge to secure themselves amidst environmental challenges. It is in regard to these needs that the desire to care for ourselves or others actually emerges in human experience. The meaning of "good," then, is completely naturalistic and empirical. The good is that which contributes to the health, survival, and maximum development of each and every living organism. Herbert Spencer was correct to at least this extent when he described the fundamental principles of what he called "life ethics": "The postulate is that life is good. Ethical conduct is that which promotes life. Evolution is good because, on the whole, it has promoted life on the whole. We can draw guidance as to how we too can promote life from [scientific information concerning] evolution."[8] Insofar as care is the basic human tendency to want to assist ourselves and others amidst the harsh challenges we confront in existence, Spencer correctly identifies the good or caring act as one that "promotes life." He also correctly draws our attention to the fact that responsible or caring action needs to be informed by whatever scientific information pertains to the strengthening of our capacities to life, to live well, and to acquire an increase in satisfaction. In this way ethics, while a normative rather than an empirical discipline, nonetheless builds upon information and theories drawn from the "public" arena of scientific investigation. Of course Spencer himself never developed a means of distinguishing between quantitative and qualitative measures of "promoting life" and hence subsequently confused "survival of the fittest" with his own tendency to advocate survival of the strongest. The key to avoiding Spencer's errors while yet preserving this important identification of the good in terms of actions that promote life lies in correctly understanding both the meaning of obligation and the difference between the "good act" and the "morally good act."

On empirical and naturalistic grounds, we seem to have an obligation to care for the needs of the ecosystem with which we are so intimately connected. Wherever there is a need or a claim for our care, there also exists obligation to meet this need or claim for care. This obligation is not just for meeting the needs of others but for "caring" for our own optimal development as well. We cannot contribute to an optimally nourishing environment unless we ourselves have developed the virtues needed to ensure strong, adaptive conduct. The concern with self-cultivation might even be considered the cornerstone of effective caring. Of course, we are but one organism of the larger ecosystem and, on empirical grounds, there is no logical reason (although surely a psychological predisposition and, in practical terms, a greater likelihood of being in a position to effect practical action) why the claims being raised by ourselves or our close kin should have any firmer hold upon our sense of obligation than those being raised by others. Again, we have an obligation wherever an organism has a need in its attempt to live, to live well, and to acquire an increase in satisfaction. William James gave succinct expression to this identification of moral obligation with whatever claims are made upon us to care when he wrote:

> Take any demand, however slight, which any creature, however weak, may make. Ought it not, for its own sake, to be satisfied? If not, prove why not.[9]

Our empirical approach to moral reasoning thus locates the "good" in any action which promotes life, contributes to the development of life, or in any way increases the range of an organism's satisfactions. The concept of obligation likewise is rooted in the actual needs and desires that arise in our experience. We have an obligation to contribute to the good for ourselves and for any other member of the ecosystem we inhabit. The only justification that we can or need to offer for identifying obligation with need-meeting is the irreducible observation that living organisms in fact make claims upon the ecosystem in which life transpires. Put another way, the only thing that confronts human consciousness as wholly unconditioned is the givenness of life (the ecosystem) itself. Everything else appears to us as conditioned and hence ultimately within our power to affect, influence, assist, or damage. The fact that the one unconditioned reality upon which our existence is predicated makes claims that are within our capacity to meet would thus certainly appear to constitute an obligation on our part.

The fact that an act contributes toward the "good" is a necessary, but not sufficient, characteristic of a moral action. Again following James, the distinction between the "good" and the "moral good" is a casuistical one. All needs cannot be met in a world of limited resources. Furthermore, many needs are incompatible with one another. An obvious example is the fact that the need of one organism to eat conflicts with the need of other organisms not to be killed. It is theoretically possible that in a world with a different physical constitution than ours, all desires, needs, and interests could be satisfied without conflict. But in our world the casuistic question of allocating priorities is most tragically practical. Decisions must be made. Limited resources must be allocated according to some criterion. Opportunities must be seized, or foregone, while they present themselves. Morality thus pertains to practical reason in its necessary task of formulating "generalized" principles whereby priorities are hierarchically ranked and organized.

Moral principles thus emerge in our effort to develop generalizations that best resolve the conflicting obligations we confront in the course of day-to-day living. While it is "good" to meet any need, the "moral" action is one that is sensitive to the larger ecosystem (inclusive of the interconnecting of generations both present and future). What distinguishes an act as moral is that it contributes to the good in ways that strengthen and nourish over time and through community. Moral rationality translates human care into a hierarchy of commitments or obligations that establishes a clear priority to those "goods" (needs, desires, interests) that contribute to the long-term benefit of individuals and the ecosystem they inhabit.

The "metaethics of care" reveals principles of moral obligation that support a rule-utilitarian approach to normative ethics. It is our obligation to help contribute to the good for ourselves and for any other organism that has an unmet need. We have already recognized, however, that all needs cannot be met nor, in fact, should they all be met. What guides this distinction between actions that contribute to the "good" and those that contribute to the "moral good" is a set of rules that help us identify which needs, desires, and interests can best be fulfilled while yet contributing to the long-term health of the larger web of life. The rules that inform moral action can be thought of as principles that are consistent with what G. G. Simpson characterized as the compositionist view of organism-environment interaction. In contrast to a reductionistic interpretation which might focus on any one organism or any one range of "goods," a compositionist understanding of the ecosystem is formulated "in terms of adaptive usefulness of structures and processes to the whole organism and to the species of which it is a part, and still further, in terms of ecological function in the communities in which the species occurs."[10] When practical reason assumes a "compositionist" form, it automatically organizes our commitments in a manner similar to that of the hypothetical "ideal observer" propounded by ethical theorists who champion the ideas of universality and justice as key ingredients of moral action. Care becomes moral, in our view, when it patterns its actions in such a way as to build an adaptive and nurturant strength, both in ourselves and in others. This kind of strength must be such as to serve the entire temporal span of our own life cycle (hence prompting us to utilize the retrospective and omniscient faculties possessed by some hypothesized "ideal observer") and to consider the requirements of the larger social and natural environments upon which our individual existence is dependent.

Care and Moral Justification

What is being argued here is that an ecological perspective softens any sharp division between empirical and normative understandings of action. Moral acts are those that can be publicly argued to be required for the care of the larger ecosystem. Empirical analysis can potentially provide us not only with information concerning the needs and desires of living organisms but also with ecological (and developmental) principles for deciding which actions are most likely to contribute to the largest sum of good over the long run. Empirical analyses can thus inform our judgments concerning those actions we "should" or "ought" to perform in our effort to care. In this way normative judgments are rooted in, and proceed in a logical fashion from, empirical understandings of the requirements of care. Antony Flew cautiously advanced this same point when he acknowledged that the naturalistic fallacy does not prohibit moral principles from having an empirical foundation.

> Morality is always supposed to be directed towards the welfare of those concerned. Now if this is indeed so, and assuming that no one's welfare could be consistent with the wholesale frustration of all his desires, it might seem that one should be able to deduce some moral conclusions from some collections of flawlessly factual premises about what is or would be desired. Certainly from premises about what people want we can hope to deduce conclusions about what would satisfy or frustrate them; while equally certainly we can, if we like, *characterize the promotion of satisfaction as moral.* Such a characterization can probably be justified both by an appeal to (much of) the common usage of the term "moral" and its associates, and also *by reference to the point and purpose of moral discourse* (emphasis added).[11]

There is, of course, a logical distinction between knowing that something is needed/desired to bring satisfaction and judging that these needs/desires should be satisfied. To blur this distinction is to commit the naturalistic fallacy of confusing empirical and normative orders of thinking. But when needs and desires are subjected to developmental and ecological principles, the casuistical task of subordinating some needs in favor of others proceeds logically and sequentially upon factual information. In fact, ecological understandings of organism-environment interaction evaluate behavior in ways that cohere with nearly every attribute that scholars such as William Frankena associate with moral thinking. For example, Frankena believes that morality is that which enhances our ability to achieve satisfaction in life by helping us to overcome the kinds of short-sightedness, egotism, or narrow vision that might otherwise impair our pursuit of satisfaction over the long run. The view of moral caring being presented here, founded as it is upon ecological perspectives, provides a framework for widening our commitments in ways that overcome precisely such egotism and short-sightedness. A "composition-ist" understanding of human action makes clear our obligation to the wider community, the future, and the nonhuman universe. Frankena also defines morality as that which prompts us to care for persons or causes beyond our immediate interests. And, too, Frankena believes that morality reveals to us a paradox in life such that when we give up our previous satisfactions in order to meet the needs of others we often find our satisfaction is restored at a new level of achievement and excellence. These are, of course, precisely the attributes we have seen that adhere to caring as it emerges and strengthens in the human ecosystem. Frankena says morality, like everything else, should be a minister to the good life—not only to one's own good life but to that of others. Therefore, morality "may restrict one in the pursuit of what is good—hence, its principles of benevolence and justice."[12] Our "anthropology of care" ministers to the good life in precisely this way, and it does so in a manner that justifies its judgments concerning benevolence and justice with reference to publicly derived understandings of "the good" and of ecological balance.

Moral judgments, emerging in the reflective efforts of practical reason, express personal commitment to fulfill the requirements of human care. The justification of these judgments is thus a function of how likely they are to meet these requirements. It is in this sense that both the natural sciences and social sciences can substantially inform our moral reflec-tions. They can help us better understand concepts such as pleasure, pain, or reinforcement. They can make us aware of our impulses and tenden-cies, many of which may foster selfish, nonmoral behavior. More importantly, they make it possible to use the notion of "health"—of the individual organism and of the larger ecosystem—as an evaluative criterion for actions. By helping us understand the factors that contribute to health and development, the sciences can help us identify those actions that predictably fulfill the requirements of care. And thus, although moral judgments always and inevitably entail an estimation of action in terms of its ability to help create an ideal environment that is not yet "out there" in any real sense, most moral dilemmas are nonetheless potentially informed by empirical knowledge concerning the cause-and-effect relationships that affect the long-term integrity of the natural and social ecosystems.

In the previous chapter we noted that the developmental psychologies of Erik Erikson and Lawrence Kohlberg revealed how concrete tasks or

challenges confronted during adulthood set people in search of generalized principles that might embody the care they wish to extend to others.
The developmental challenges confronted in adult life disturb the cognitive equilibriums or patterns of organism-environment interaction that
were acquired earlier and make possible the personal acquisition of what
Kohlberg describes as a "fully-principled" level of moral reasoning. In
Kohlberg's words,

> From my developmental perspective, moral principles *are active
> reconstructions of experience;* the recognition that moral judgment
> demands a universal form is neither a universal a priori intuition of
> humanity nor a peculiar invention by a philosopher but, rather, a
> portion of the universal reconstruction of judgment in the process of
> development.[13]

What I wish to emphasize is that our anthropology of care sees concepts
such as benevolence, universality, logical comprehensiveness, and justice
as "brain-born" hypotheses engendered by practical rationality in its
efforts to extend care to the larger ecosystem. Thus, whereas Kohlberg
places emphasis upon the cognitive structure underlying fully principled
moral thought (i.e., that it display reversibility of perspectives, universality, and logical comprehensiveness), we are trying to draw attention to the
prior web of relationships and competing "goods" that prompt practical
reason to find principles for generalized caring. Moral justification, in our
view, rests not in the cognitive structure of generalized caring per se, but
rather in the larger anthropological function of practical reason's efforts
to order competing nonmoral goods into an adaptively sound pattern.
Moral obligation thus rests in the need of finite organisms to meet their
own and others' needs, interests, and desires. Concepts such as benevolence, justice, reversibility, and universality are theoretical strategies by
which practical reason seeks to translate caring into "generalized caring."
It follows that the view of morality being presented here, although
based on naturalistic understandings of the "good," is nonetheless a
noncognitivist one (albeit of a "soft" variety in that it allows for clear and
meaningful discussion of moral "hypotheses"). A moral judgment has the
character of a hypothesis which, while built upon and subject to critical
reformulation according to empirical evidence, itself claims only heuristic
utility. A moral judgment is an estimate of how we might best go about
caring in light of our ever-expanding conception of some ideal environment in which a maximum number of needs and interests have been
satisfied. Moral rationality thus has to do with the bold commitment to
pattern our actions so as to conform to some ideal "ecosystem" which is
not "out there" in any simple or straightforward sense. Particular

judgments concerning the form of care that will best minister to the good (considered in terms of this ideal ecosystem) have the character of biological mutations or free variations. We can trust, then, that the environment itself will ultimately exert redressive pressure upon our practical rationality to organize and reorganize our commitments in ever more sensitive ways.

Because our moral principles emerge amidst the ongoing tasks of practical reason, the "pragmatist" view of morality presented here is subjectivist, but not necessarily individualistic or anthropocentric. Viewed within our anthropology of care, moral valuing is an activity of human subjects. As Anthony Weston notes, "even if only human beings value in this sense, it does not follow that only human beings have value; it does not follow that human beings must be the sole or final objects of valuation. Subjectivism does not imply, so to say, subject-centrism; our actual values can be much more complex and world-directed."[14] To avoid such subject-centrism, obviously we must remain sensitive to each new claim as it arises within ourselves, from others, or from the natural universe. We must also continuously revise our conceptions of the good and the strategies best used to create this good as new information is uncovered by the natural sciences, the social sciences, and the various "helping professions" such as psycho-therapy and the ministry. As William James expressed it, in its efforts to care, practical rationality must always wait on facts:

> [Practical reason] must bide its time, and be ready to revise its conclusions from day to day. [The individual] knows that he must vote always for the richer universe, for the good which seems most organizable, most fit to enter into complex combinations, most apt to be a member of a more inclusive whole. But which particular universe this is he cannot know for certain in advance.[15]

Implicit in James's view is the recognition that in an evolving universe there are no such things as static moral truths. The "truth" of a moral principle is ultimately a function of its ability to give rise to a "richer universe." It follows that moral integrity is not so much an issue of perma-nent convictions as it is one of character. Moral integrity rests primarily in the strenuousness of our commitment to care and to care effectively.

Care and the Strenuous Life

The evolution now affecting the future of the human species is influenced far less by genetic variations than it is by changes in our acquired behaviors and ideas, that is, in culture. The "zone" in which this evolution transpires is the zone of individual decisions and the effect these decisions have upon the welfare of the larger ecosystem. The blight of modern carelessness—urban slums, wholesale pollution, eroded educational systems, and the threat of nuclear self-destruction—points to an ominous future that will not easily forgive us if we are too weak hearted or morally incapable of making necessary sacrifices on the ecosystem's behalf.

Our anthropology of care is important not only because it can address metaethical issues in ways that permit public, empirically based discussion, but also because it is able to address the cultural and psychological factors influencing our individual willingness to adopt a moral outlook. It was in this context that William James observed that the deepest difference, practically, in the moral life of human beings "is the difference between the easy-going and the strenuous mood. When in the easy-going mood the shrinking from present ill is our ruling consideration. The strenuous mood, on the contrary, makes us quite indifferent to present ill, if only the greater ideal be attained."[16] The strenuous mood directs our attention to the requirements of moral obligation. People, of course, are ridden with conflicting impulses and instinctual tendencies—most of which side with the selfish comforts of the easy-going mood. The strenuous mood exists, at least in part, in the psychological capacity to envision "the greater ideal" and to hold this ideal firmly in our awareness so that it imparts a direction to our action. As James wrote, "If a brief definition of ideal or moral action were required, none could be given which would better fit the appearances than this: It is action in the line of the greatest resistance."[17] The strenuous mood, then, seeks to resist the tendency to seek immediate gratification and instead to ensure that conduct be aimed at securing long-range health for oneself and one's larger community.

For James, the strenuous mood is a potential in every human being. To become activated and to predominate over carelessness, however, the strenuous mood requires a supporting cultural climate. For example, it requires a culture that provides emotionally rejuvenating experiences. Individuals from time to time need what James called "moral holidays" during which they are free to enjoy their own immediate experience without inhibitions imposed by the larger community. Various forms of religious "inwardness" are one such mechanism whereby individuals might temporarily let go of concern with worldly obligations and become inwardly nourished.[18] The experience of direct contact with nature is yet another means whereby individuals might have their inner life quickened and their moral sensibilities sharpened.

Important in itself, as well as in anticipation of the themes that will dominate the next chapter of this book, is the relationship James detected between our religious or philosophical beliefs and the psychological capacity for the strenuous mood. James was aware that a strictly humanistic understanding of morality emphasizes our obligation to the future. Realistically, however, the needs of some future society are really too remote and too far removed from our daily concerns to elicit strenuous care. As James put it, most of us "do not love these [people] of the future keenly enough. . . . [We are not psychologically capable] of agonizing ourselves or making others agonize for these good creatures just at present."[19] It is at this point we become acutely aware of Erikson's description of how each of us seizes upon some ideology (i.e., philosophy or religion) to give shape and direction to our emerging identity. A strictly materialistic ideology will foreshorten the range within which we identify our commitments. Yet, at least certain types of religious belief make clear to us that we have an obligation to a wider community and to the moral judgment of the future. In James's words, "When, however, we believe that a God is there and that he is one of the claimants, the infinite perspective opens out. . . . The more imperative ideals now begin to speak with an altogether new objectivity and significance. . . . Every sort of energy and endurance, of courage and capacity for handling life's evils, is set free in those who have religious faith. For this reason the strenuous type of character will on the battle-field of human history always outwear the easygoing type, and religion will drive irreligion to the wall."[20]

The strenuous mood is aroused in us by the "wilder passions" that accentuate the need for self-sacrifice and for commitment. In this sense religious belief is more—not less—rational than either atheism or agnosticism. Understanding that the function of practical reason is to facilitate effective adaptation, then "of two conceptions equally fit to satisfy the logical demand, the one which awakens the active impulses, or satisfies other aesthetic demands better than the other, will be accounted the more rational conception, and will deservedly prevail."[21] But, for James, the theistic beliefs of the majority of the American church-going public are not nearly so "rational" in this expanded sense of the term. Belief in an all-knowing, all-powerful Supreme Being can actually foster indifference and moral passivity. The biblical imagery of a god who presides over the universe from above and occasionally intervenes in human affairs through a miraculous act tends to elicit a false confidence that a Supreme Being—not us—will take all the action that is necessary in our world. Much of conventional piety fosters an irrational approach to life's most serious dilemmas and, perhaps even worse, tends to convey the mistaken notion that this world is here to be exploited by human ingenuity.

Against the kinds of religious belief that reinforce the easygoing mood, James posed a religious philosophy built squarely upon the empirical data supplied by direct religious experience and upon certain inferences drawn from the evolutionary process whereby life has developed and flourished on this planet. According to James, the strenuous mood is most likely to be aroused by an understanding of a finite God who is an active force, but not the only force, in our evolving universe. James's view, which is similar to what today is called "panentheism," focuses upon God as the immanent spiritual power that expresses itself through the creative movement of nature. In this view we are literally connected with God's creative life and, in fact, are the "leading shoot" of God's activity upon this planet. It is we who have the responsibility of carrying the life process forward. Real gains and real losses are at stake in the way we conduct ourselves and shape the outcome of the evolutionary process. Don Browning has summarized this connection between the strenuous mood and belief in a finite God—a connection that expresses itself in a pluralistic (i.e., where God is the chief, but not the sole, causal power) universe—by noting how James

> contrasts the "belief that the world is still in the process of making" with the belief that there is an "eternal edition" of the world "ready-made and complete." The idea that the world is still in the process of being made is the one that is consistent with James's pluralism and pragmatism. James believes that both pluralism and monism confirm our strenuous moods; but, as James writes, "Pluralism actually demands them, since it makes the world's salvation depend upon the energizing of its several parts, among which we are."[22]

We will put this religious perspective concerning moral obligation aside until the next chapter. It remains for us to emphasize, however, that the unfinished and evolving character of our universe demands that we learn to translate our care into effective action. Misguided conduct, no matter what our inner intention, is not really caring conduct. Raising children, distributing wealth within a society, providing for basic human needs with public programs that do not perpetuate the problems they were designed to alleviate, and enriching lives through the creation of consumer goods without doing irreversible damage to the environment—all of these require technical skill every bit as much as a well-meaning heart. The strenuousness of real care includes an overt, active, and knowledgeable understanding of what leads to healthy development in the psychological, cultural, economic, and political realms. We must engage strenuously in the public policy debates that determine how responsibly we will care for our world. As Robert Bellah and his colleagues have pointed out so poignantly, there are "habits of the American heart" that have prevented our public decisions from expressing true care and are threatening the very fabric of our culture. These "habits" are the countless ways in which we confuse individualism with the avoidance of commitment to the common good. "We have committed what to the republican founders of our nation was the cardinal sin: we have put our own good, as individuals, as groups, as a nation, ahead of the common good."[23] We have fashioned American individualism around the easygoing rather than the strenuous mood and in the process have eroded our own capacity to care effectively for the world about us.

On a Certain Blindness in Human Beings

The view of ethics that is presented here might well be called an ethics of appreciation. That is, it roots caring action in our ability to perceive and respond to the needs and interests arising in our environment. It follows that a major stumbling block to the moral life of caring is our failure to perceive or appreciate adequately the needs of other persons or other species. Thus the "blindness" that pertains to our nature as caring beings is the blindness with which we are all afflicted in regard to the feelings or needs of those who are different from ourselves. The practical nature of human rationality causes us to become absorbed in our own limited functions and duties. This concern with our own lives blinds us to persons or causes that are remote from our immediate interests. As a consequence we become indifferent and mistakenly enshrine our own desires and interests as criteria of truth or merit. William James observed that the recognition of this certain blindness in human beings should force upon us the moral relevance of certain attitudinal virtues:

> It absolutely forbids us to be forward in pronouncing on the meaninglessness of forms of existence other than our own; and it commands us to tolerate, respect, and indulge those whom we see harmlessly interested and happy in their own ways, however unintelligible these may be to us. Hands off: neither the whole of truth nor the whole of good is revealed to any single observer.[24]

Because of this tendency toward moral blindness, our ethics of care might reasonably be argued to include at least two additional and derivative principles of obligation. Since moral obligation resides in meeting those claims actually being made by living organisms (or the "living planet" that sustains these organisms), it follows that it would also be our duty never to kill, injure, or in any other way limit an individual organism's capacity to express life for reasons extrinsic to the requirements of an ideally healthy ecosystem. A second duty would be that of preventing prejudice or personal rigidity from preventing concrete demands and claims from reaching our full awareness. This implies, of course, that the claims of any and all individuals, regardless of race, sex, national origin, or creed, are equally binding upon us in our duty to fulfill the requirements of care. This also implies that there are no needs or claims that can be predetermined on a priori grounds as incommensurate with our moral obligation. No one of us knows in advance what aesthetic tastes, life-styles, or ideas of the good life will most readily contribute to the objective and subjective enrichment of life on this planet. This principle of nonprejudicial openness to others also applies to the nonhuman world, as William James suggested in his query, "Take any demand, however slight, which any creature, however weak, may make. Ought it not, for its own sake, to be satisfied?" In short, empathy and nonprejudicial sensitivity to the needs of others would be virtues indispensable to the moral life.

There is another dimension of "this certain blindness" of human beings. Psychologist C. Daniel Batson has given serious attention to the question, "Are we capable of caring for anyone other than ourselves?" In a series of experiments he found that what distinguishes behavior that is genuinely other-regarding from that which is self-serving (even though it might be "disguised" to look like altruistic action) is the presence of empathy for the person or object toward which we are acting. In Batson's words, "our capacity for altruistic caring is limited to those for whom we feel empathy. In study after study, when empathy for the person in need is low, the pattern of helping suggests underlying egoistic motivation."[25]

Batson's studies on the role of empathy in overcoming moral blindness suggest that we need to pay close attention to those factors that prevent us from having nonegoistic identification with others. One such barrier to the development of empathy for others is the general lack of healthy narcissism among modern Americans. It is impossible to love others if we do not genuinely love ourselves. As we noted in chapter 2 in our discussion of early psychological development, human beings require consistent and warm relationships with valued others in order to feel that they are prized and intrinsically worthy of love. When people lack such sustained "mutuality" with others they come to feel unworthy of love and develop what is usually described as "pathological narcissism"—a condition that prompts them to protect themselves against further psychological injury by creating emotional barriers that will isolate them from the give and take of interpersonal relationships. Pathological narcissism is also characterized by continuous efforts to manipulate others and an inability to consider other persons in their own right.

Our culture has underestimated the importance of the kind of healthy self-love that comes from receiving warmth and affection from those around us. Healthy self-esteem makes it possible to feel inherently connected to the world around us and to be capable of venturing out into life free from crippling defensiveness. Individuals who have a deep sense of "mutuality" with others are psychologically capable of having empathy or active resonance with the world about them. Importantly, there are also forms of spirituality that promote the experience of mutuality with a religious "Other" and, in so doing, help us overcome that certain blindness in human beings. An ethic of care presupposes the psychological capacity for attending to and valuing the welfare of others. And hence a culture that seeks to promote caring behavior must foster the kinds of mutuality that make empathy possible.

Our inquiry into the moral or ethical dimension of care thus prompts us to rephrase our original question, Who cares? Understood in moral terms, we might better ask, Who cares effectively? Moral reflection upon the tasks we are presented with in the course of everyday life suggests that the person who cares effectively is one who engages life in the strenuous mood. The person who cares effectively is one who is willing to pattern his or her action in accordance with those rules of conduct most likely to meet the requirements of an ideally nurturing environment. The caring person is one who is genuinely other-regarding, who perceives and responds to the larger ecosystem in an empathic, nonprejudicial way. He or she acts in ways that will strengthen, both in themselves and in others, a developing capacity for the healthy expression of life.

4

Caring as Participation
in the Divine Life

*

IN CHAPTER 2 we noted that developmental challenges confronted in adulthood often entail the effort to discover our place in the greater scheme of things. When Carl Jung observed that of his patients over thirty-five, "all have been people whose problem in the last resort was that of finding a religious outlook on life," he was referring to adults' overarching need to understand how their lives participate in something of intrinsic meaning. Nearly every emotional or intellectual challenge adults face can be understood as spiritual in the broadest sense of the term. This is particularly true of our moral "struggles." Even the fully mature personality must confront the ambiguity concerning any decision to forego simple hedonism in favor of moral commitments. It was in this context that Lawrence Kohlberg pointed out how his studies of moral development indicated that "the answer to the question 'Why be moral?' at this level entails the question 'Why live?' (and the parallel question, 'How face death?') so that ultimate moral maturity requires a mature solution to the question of the meaning of life."[1] Sustained reflection on who or what we should care for raises issues that are thus not resolvable on purely logical grounds. These issues are ontological (i.e., pertaining to the intrinsic structures of being) and religious.

Our attempt to understand the "anthropology of care" leads to issues that are themselves insusceptible to scientific analysis. We might ask, for example, what is implied by a creation that has given rise to beings such as ourselves who have the power to direct the entire future of life on this planet? Or, what does our role as the conscious directors of evolution imply about our relationship to the ultimate power that gave rise to the universe? The way we answer such questions reveals our deepest assumptions about the nature and meaning of life. These assumptions concerning just how or why life is constructed the way it is also bear directly upon our willingness to care for causes outside our own immediate interests. The personality theorist Gordon Allport understood this connection well when he wrote that "ethical standards are difficult to sustain without idealism; and idealism is difficult to sustain without a myth of Being."[2] "Myths of Being" differ greatly in their identification of the needs, interests, and satisfactions we ought to care about. The final argument of this book is that the most strenuous form of care is rooted in a religious vision of life and, for that matter, a very particular kind of religious vision.

Religious Thought and Human Experience

It should be clear from the outset that religious thinking is not necessarily the same as theology. Theology is a subset of religious thinking. Whereas religious thought is potentially limitless in its form or substance, theology assumes the a priori validity of a particular religious tradition. The scriptures, doctrines, and ecclesiastical heritage of that tradition are taken as normative and either explained or justified in terms of the contemporary cultural situation. Put another way, the basic definitions and limits of theological discussion are laid down by the "theological circle" of authoritative symbols and creeds within which the theologian operates. This is the case whether the theological tradition happens to be Buddhist, Hindu, Jewish, Christian, or Muslim. New insights and new applications surely arise from time to time, but the "theological circle" itself is more or less a closed one.

Religious thinking, in contrast, is not necessarily undertaken within a theological circle. The essential task of religious thinking is to orient individuals to the broadest range of experience, to describe what experience testifies to be its ultimate context, and to induce the appropriate existential and ethical response.[3] As William Clebsch defines it, religious thought represents "the reasoned, the cogent, and the evocative considerations of ways in which the human spirit . . . seriously and strenuously relates itself to nature, to society, and to deity."[4] Religious thought therefore need have no a priori normative "circle" other than human experience itself. Its task is to focus our attention upon what might be called the "limit dimension" of human experience.[5] And, in contrast to theology that aims for systematic and internally consistent doctrines, religious thought can be content with distilling images and metaphors from human experience that reveal partial glimpses of the metaphysical ground out of which life arises.

While religious thought is not science, it is, at its best, co-scientific. Its basic images are those born of human experience and for this reason these images can be interpreted scientifically or religiously. Scientifically interpreted, these images (i.e., sense perceptions) are expected to yield information concerning material causation that will lead to prediction and control. Religiously interpreted, these images are expected to yield an insight into that which lies "beyond the limit" of finite reason in a manner that induces ethical dedication and a particular mode of life orientation. Thus, while grounded in and continuously guided by empirical knowledge concerning human experience, religious thinking is not empirical in the same sense as science. It is better to think of religious thinking as a kind of creative construction of existence derived from those "limit" experiences in which we—however vaguely—discern the ultimate or metaphysical meaning of our existence. For this reason it is inappropriate to demand that religious intuitions be subjected to the tests of verification and falsification that science demands of its propositions.[6] Yet religious thinking would lose its validity, or at the very least become obsolete, if the essential experiences or imagery it utilizes were in some way to lose their significance in a culture's scientific outlook. Put differently, good metaphysics must be predicated upon good physics.

Religious thought potentially transforms our experience of the world in ways that yield some insight into the great questions that confront humans in their effort to find meaning in life. Religious thinking points scientific or experiential information in the direction of faith. The word faith, here, does not imply commitment to beliefs that are completely irrational or contrary to science. Indeed, religion shares with science an intention to accumulate knowledge that will better enable humanity to adapt to the larger environment. Where religious thinking differs from scientific thinking is that it postulates that our highest fulfillment requires our "adaptation" to a power or intelligence that is in some way central to all existence—God. An empirically based religious faith tries to build upon a culture's understandings of successful adaptation in ways that accommodate this conviction concerning the presence and causal efficacy of a metaphysical reality that lies outside the domain of scientific analysis. What distinguishes the interpretative perspective in which religion "constructs" human experience is its intuition that this "more" beyond or outside the physical universe has a significance for our lives and that our highest good comes from bringing our lives and actions into some kind of harmony with this ultimate context of experience. The intention underlying religious thought is thus to fashion "adaptive strategies" that are not less than scientific but more than scientific. It seeks to intuit an ultimate meaning in life such that all human activities can be understood as deriving their particular significance according to how fully they contribute to, or participate in, this overarching meaning.

It is in this larger sense of religious thought that evolutionary biologist

Ernst Mayr wrote that "virtually all biologists are religious, in the deeper sense of this word, even though it may be a religion without revelation. . . . The unknown and maybe unknowable instills in us a sense of humility and awe."[7] The experiential awe before the "more" of existence stimulates our fundamental drive to understand the meaning of this evolving universe. Evolutionary theorist Arthur Peacocke has commented that

> the scientifically reductionist account has a limited range and needs to be incorporated into a larger theistic framework that has been constructed in response to questions of the kind, Why is there anything at all? and What kind of universe must it be if insentient matter can evolve naturally into self-conscious, thinking persons? and What is the meaning of personal life in such a cosmos?[8]

Scientists, qua scientists, are unlikely to seek such incorporation insofar as the scientific method restricts its scope of inquiry in ways that exclude such questions. Inquiry into these kinds of questions is more akin to aesthetics than science. It seeks to intuit, appreciate, and evoke response to a dimension of experience that cuts beneath the subject-object sphere of sensory and rational analysis. The aesthetic sensibility of religious reflection probes the limit dimension of human experience. By this I mean that it pushes at the boundaries or barriers of life as apprehended by the rational intellect. Thought becomes distinctively religious when it probes scientific conceptions of causality for hints of the operation of a final or ultimate cause. Scientific analysis is properly concerned with the material and efficient causes of events that transpire in the universe. It is the very nature of science to look for the material or efficient causes of events and to assume what might be called a "physical determinism." Attempts to consider the possible role of final (i.e., owing to purpose, goal-direction, intention) or ultimate (i.e., owing to the agency of some extramundane spiritual agency) causes are nonscientific. Yet, humans nonetheless ask such questions, and some of the most profound moral and psychological challenges we face in life revolve around our efforts to address such issues as the purpose or spiritual meaning of our lives. Religious thought is the effort to educe these kinds of intrinsic meaning from factual accounts of the universe. It seeks to detect significance and direction in the very universe that science, qua science, can only describe as random or devoid of any ultimate purpose.

It is possible to identify a continuing strain of religious thought that has helped shape and guide American culture in its pursuit of ultimate meanings. Constituting what Clebsch refers to as an "aesthetic spiritual-ity," this tradition has much to offer our contemporary efforts to elucidate the ultimate contexts of our efforts to care for one another.

Existing outside the theological circle inhabited by our nation's churches, the proponents of this aesthetic spirituality have identified true spirituality neither with conventional moral piety nor with adherence to scriptural or doctrinal creeds. They have instead sought to point out the ways in which we might behold God as spiritually present within the natural universe and to evoke in us "a consciousness of the beauty of living in harmony with divine things."[9]

When Ralph Waldo Emerson declared that "nature is the symbol of spirit," he laid the foundation of American aesthetic spirituality.[10] Nature, he proclaimed, is "the organ through which the universal spirit speaks to the individual and strives to lead back the individual to it."[11] Emerson frequently referred to God or the universal spirit as the Over-Soul. The Over-Soul is an immanent force or principle working through nature and ever available to the open or receptive mind. It was Emerson's conviction that a receptive stance toward nature permits "an influx of Divine Mind into our mind."[12] By entering into nonegoistic states of consciousness we all have the capacity to behold directly "that divine principle that lurks within."[13] In this way Emerson was anchoring religious conviction neither in scripture nor in church attendance, but in distinct modes of human experience. The moment in which we open up to the Over-Soul's activity in nature is, for Emerson, marked by "that shudder of awe and delight with which the individual soul always mingles with the Universal Soul."[14] The self, having opened up to nature's depths, is instantaneously "filled with the divinity which flows through all things."[15]

Emerson believed that an aesthetic spirituality of this kind has a transformative influence upon our psychological makeup. It makes possible a direct participation in the creative activities of the universal spirit. Psychologically considered, consciousness of the universal spirit within or behind our individual lives enables us to transcend environmental determinisms and to become freer, more creative—in short, to be truly self-reliant. Understanding God as the "divinity which flows through all things," there is no final distinction between authentic self-reliance and God-reliance. The "self" that is the source of authentic self-reliance is not the self whose identity is determined through the socialization process. It is, rather, the self that has placed the rational ego in temporary abeyance so as to become receptive to the "exertions of a power which exists not in time, or space, but an instantaneous in-streaming causing power."[16] Emerson's major contribution to American religious thought was thus a recognition that each and every human being has the potential to recognize, and to respond to, the directive activity of the universal spirit as it operates throughout nature. Of course, Emerson lived before the Darwinian revolution in science and before industrialization made the dangers of "American carelessness" fully known. But he did draw our attention to the religious significance of becoming receptive to the depths of nature and of the transformative character of opening ourselves to the "currents of the Universal Being."

William James picked up the Emersonian strand of American religious thought and developed it in ways that squared fully with the empiricist foundations of modern science. He did so by arguing that the narrow empiricism associated with what might be called "scientism" fails to do justice to the full range of human experience. Conversely, a "radical empiricism" can do justice to the demands of both our scientific and spiritual temperaments. Radical empiricism, unlike the narrower empiricism of scientism, does not demand that all of its discoveries be capable of replication: all human experiences cannot be precisely duplicated. To be radical, an empiricism must never admit into its formulations any element that has not been directly experienced, nor can it exclude any element that has been experienced. This dictum requires including as "primary data" not only the various objects of experience but also the various experiences of relatedness or connectedness that an experience entails.[17] Considering "conjunctive relations" among the data furnished by an empiricist approach to life has profound implications for moral and religious philosophy. It takes seriously our sense of relatedness to a "more" from which we sense that life derives its ultimate meaning. James believed that a radical empiricism can do justice to the metaphysical insights contained in religious or mystical experience. It takes seriously our experience of a "conjunctive relation" to the ultimate source of order and creativity in the universe. He wrote, "The further limits of our being plunge, it seems to me, into an altogether other dimension of existence from the sensible and merely 'understandable' world. . . . I will call this higher part of the universe by the name of God. We and God have business with each other; and in opening ourselves to [God's] influence our deepest destiny is fulfilled."[18] Importantly, James understood the nature of the "business" we share with God in ways that highlight the critical importance of the strenuous mood in directing the future of our evolving universe. And, for this reason, the type of spirituality advocated by James and Emerson can guide us in our attempt to understand the religious dimensions of caring action in our age.

Religion and Practical Reason in a Nuclear Age

The threat of a nuclear holocaust gives succinct expression to the horrors of modern carelessness. The distinct possibility of the nuclear destruction of our planet symbolizes the countless ways in which human behavior threatens to undermine the very possibility of life on earth. The pollution of our water, the poisoning of the atmosphere, the strain upon resources created by overpopulation, and the rapid proliferation of carcinogenic materials all testify to the ecological crisis jeopardizing the future of our world. Because the nuclear destruction of our planet is still potentially avoidable, it is probably not as deserving of our dire attention as the irreversible ecological damage we have already set into motion. Yet, because nuclear weaponry represents a more dramatic and instantaneous form of self-destruction, it serves as a symbol of the most urgent issues of our age. Harvard theologian Gordon Kaufman has poignantly described the ways in which our nuclear age has established a new agenda for responsible religious reflection. All language about God and the "business" we and God have with each other must be framed in terms of "the momentous change in the human religious situation brought about by the possibility that we humans, by ourselves, will utterly destroy not only ourselves but our species, all future generations, thus bringing the entire human project, through which and for which many hundreds of generations have labored, to an abrupt and final halt."[19]

The perilous condition of our nuclear age reveals the inadequacy of the Western biblical tradition for guiding human conduct in its most inclusive contexts. True, the Bible frequently speaks of the end of the world. But it does so in the context of God's own action in bringing about the final judgment through which God will separate the wheat from the chaff. In fact, many Americans view the impending catastrophe from either nuclear self-destruction or ecological upheaval as somehow God's will and God's doing. Others dismiss the seriousness of the situation by proclaiming that in the final hour Christ will return in the clouds and save his chosen flock from this disastrous fate. Both of these responses is consistent with biblical theology, which admonishes us to be obedient to the divine will and await God's decisive intervention in the world. But, as Kaufman points out,

> in focusing this way on God's activity, both of these interpretations obscure what is central and novel in this potential event as it confronts us today, namely, that it will be we human beings who are absolutely and fully responsible if this catastrophe occurs, that this event confronts us primarily as an act of human doing rather than of divine will, and that both our actions and our hopes with respect to it, therefore, must be directed toward the transformation of our human institutions and policies.[20]

It will not be sufficient for "progressive theologians" to analyze the current cultural situation in light of the basic claims of the biblical tradition. To seek some new application of age-old doctrines is to continue to limit ourselves to terms and concepts that simply lack the empirical foundations to guide practical reason in effective ways. This is why Kaufman suggests that we should instead ground modern religious thought in our knowledge concerning

> the sources and sustaining powers from whence we come. Human life today is generally understood to be an expression of, and to be continually sustained by, the great web of life which has gradually emerged and evolved on planet earth. . . . Human existence, as we understand it today, could never have come into being apart from this long process of differentiation and development. We humans must understand ourselves in the first place, therefore, as one strand in the very ancient and complex web of life, a strand, moreover, which would not exist apart from this context which has brought it forth and which continues to sustain it at every point.[21]

Religious thought, in other words, must return to a self-consciously empirical mode of reflection. It must locate the ultimate context of our moral and religious commitments within—not outside—the great web of life that has gradually emerged and evolved on planet earth.

The function of religious thought in the life of practical reason is much like that of any other set of hypotheses generated in the "middle loop" of thought. The distinctive purpose of religious thought, as we noted above, is to orient us to the broadest ranges of human experience and to induce the appropriate existential and ethical response to what confronts as ultimate. Religious thought functions in a manner that is somewhat between the dogmatic certainty of absolutist theology and the anxious uncertainty of complete agnosticism. That is, religious thought, like agnosticism, utilizes an empirical method that knows of no final certainties; in particular, it makes no claim to know what Being or God is like independent of its involvement in our universe.[22] Yet, this same empirical orientation allows religious thought to claim some knowledge of the tendencies or purposes of Being as it manifests itself in the physical and psychological process of life and to discern certain norms for our existential and ethical response; it does so, however, through reflection upon the data furnished by radical empiricism, not through scriptural exegesis.

When reason is understood in its full evolutionary-adaptive sense, it becomes clear that religious belief is not only a rational form of thought but actually the most rational form of thought. That is, at least potentially, religious thought facilitates the kind of ecologically sensitive conduct that promotes the aim of organisms to live, to live well, and to gain an increase in satisfaction. Religious faith buttresses our confidence that the universe is essentially melioristic or capable of improvement. Practical reason, seeking continuously to promote the "good" (for ourselves and others) within a resisting natural and social environment, cannot operate effectively without some implicit confidence that a higher order of good can indeed be achieved. The hardships, losses, and suffering produced in our finite world constantly threaten to undermine our belief in the melioristic character of the world. Affirming that the world is not utterly indifferent or opposed to our efforts is a broadly spiritual and courageous act. Without such faith in even the chance that reality will be receptive to our efforts, we are unlikely to act with energy or conviction. Religious belief stimulates practical reason by providing it with confidence that even "evils" can become tributary to the good and that there is a power central to existence that is receptive to our efforts on behalf of the miracle of life.

Because religious thought—at least that of the aesthetic variety—orients our actions in service of the "divinity flowing through all things," it awakens in us the strenuous mood as does no other form of thought. As James noted of the transformation in our psychological constitution created by religious belief, "At a single stroke it changes the dead blank *it* of the world into a living *thou,* with whom the whole man may have dealings."[23] Religious interpretations of experience strengthen our sense of connectedness with the universe and in this way help us to overcome the certain moral blindness in human nature. James concluded that on strictly anthropological grounds "we are obliged, on account of their extraordinary influence upon action and endurance, to class [religious beliefs] among the most important biological functions of mankind."[24] It is a simple fact that the "hypothesis of God" works in human experience and is, on pragmatic grounds, consistent with practical rationality. Yet religious beliefs vary in the kind of practical rationality they give rise to. Different religious systems "make pragmatically different ethical appeals."[25] The task of religious thought, then, is to "build out" our religious beliefs in ways that will combine satisfactorily with all the other working truths that will guide us to a larger, richer, more satisfying life.

God and Evolution

Historical perspective reveals how fully humans shape and reshape their conceptions of God to illuminate what they perceive to be the ultimate principle at work in the universe. Once established, however, theological traditions tend to de-emphasize the human role in creating their most fundamental symbols and instead speak of the "revealed" status of the doctrines they inherited from earlier generations. But the academic study of religion proves conclusively that humans define God in ways that evoke ethical and existential responses appropriate to their own historical or cultural epoch. In the West, we have inherited conceptions of God that previous generations described as a Universal Ruler or King who, though demanding our devotion, permits us to gratify ourselves and to exploit the environment as much as possible. These religious metaphors have proved to be an inadequate foundation for guiding practical reason. The ecological essayist Wendell Berry put this succinctly when he maintained that "the great disaster of human history is one that happened to or within religion: that is, the conceptual division between the holy and the world, the excerpting of the Creator from the creation."[26] In more "primitive religions" god (or gods) was more intimately bound up with nature and stimulated veneration for it. But in monotheism deity is elevated far beyond our earth. In this way it becomes possible to fear and worship God without fearing or worshiping nature; indeed, it becomes possible to love God while hating his creation. As Berry puts it,

> If God was not in the world, then obviously the world was a thing of inferior importance, or of no importance at all. Those who were disposed to exploit it were thus free to do so. And this split in public attitudes was inevitably mirrored in the lives of individuals: a man could aspire to heaven with his mind and his heart while destroying the earth and his fellow men, with his hands.[27]

We will take it as an established fact that all images of God are, and always have been, drawn from those patterns of human experience that strike us as most capable of disclosing the ultimate reference point for our existential and moral orientation. The critical task of religious thinking, then, is determining just which patterns of experience give rise to metaphors or models of the divine that will best nourish our collective efforts to live, to live well, and to gain an increase in our satisfaction. Our American heritage of aesthetic spirituality, particularly in its Jamesian formulation, is here well suited to our religious needs. James finally eschewed both conventional monotheism and the simple monism found in popular mysticism. Both, he maintained, foster moral passivity and an ostrichlike intellectual outlook that ignores the findings of scientific study. Instead, James advocated that both the empirical structure of religious experience and an aesthetic reading of evolutionary biology support what he termed "a pluralistic panpsychic view of the universe."[28]

It is important that we understand what James meant both by "panpsychism" and by "pluralism" as attributes of the presence of God in our evolving universe. Panpsychism claims that matter—at all levels—

contains an inner, psychic, or spiritual dimension. Panpsychism insists that matter be viewed consistently from a cosmological perspective. Which is to say that the natural order should be seen as in some fundamental sense expressing the creative aims of the First Cause. Panpsychism differs from monism or pantheism in that it does not imply that God or the First Cause is "nothing but" the world of nature. Panpsychism is compatible with the twentieth-century notion of "panentheism," whereby God is understood as fully immersed with—yet also in some way transcending—the evolutionary process. The important claim being advanced by the concept of panpsychism is that from a cosmological perspective we can make no rigid distinction between God and nature, or between spirit and matter. It also suggests that there is a sacredness and ultimacy to the whole of the universe—both in its human and nonhuman expressions.

The panpsychic element of James's religious vision stems directly from the aesthetic sensibility that he shared with Emerson. James fervently maintained that a radical empiricism must count the "more" of religious or mystical experience among the dimensions of the real. A radical empiricism is one that recognizes the existence of "ranges of life . . . that naturalism with its literal and legal virtues never recks of."[29] What James intended here was to link the American pragmatic tradition with philosophical romanticism. In a lineage that stretches through Hegel, Henri Bergson, Samuel Alexander, Alfred North Whitehead, and the so-called "empirical" theologians such as Bernard Loomer, Schubert Ogden, and Charles Hartshorne, James stretched empiricism to detect the ongoing creative activity of the First Cause in and through all other material causes. In this vision, evolution itself becomes the process whereby the "more" continually gives rise to new and more complex forms of life. Such, in fact, is the view anthropologist Loren Eisley assumes when he reflects upon the marvel of evolution.

> I would say that if "dead" matter has reared up this curious landscape of fiddling crickets, song sparrows, and wondering men, it must be plain even to the most devoted materialist that the matter of which he speaks contains amazing, if not dreadful powers, and may not impossibly be, as Hardy has suggested, "but one mask of many worn by the Great Face behind."[30]

God, or the "more" of experience, can in this way be understood as the final or ultimate cause that works through the material and efficient causes identified by our natural and social sciences. This is not to confuse religious propositions with scientific assertions. Religious propositions are imaginative or metatheoretical constructions. References to the existence or activity of God are not descriptions of the nature or structure of existence per se. They do not, therefore, convey factual knowledge about our sensory world in the manner science does. Nor are they subject to experimental verification or falsification in the way that scientific findings are. But "imaginative constructions" of experience are nonetheless necessary to all human mental or psychological functioning. And, more importantly, the adaptive activities of practical reason are most comprehensively served when these imaginative constructions assume a religious or metaphysical form. Responsible religious reflection assumes that some attempts to "build out" our religious intuitions will cohere with empirical data better than others and thus that some religious reflections can be expected to produce more significant types of ethical and existential response than others.

It is incumbent upon those who engage in sustained religious thought today to understand the ways in which the symbol "God" illuminates our understanding of the evolutionary process. Gordon Kaufman, for example, maintains that the word *god* is a symbol for "a reality, an ultimate tendency or power, which is working itself out in an evolutionary process that has produced not only myriads of living species, but also at least one living form able to shape and transform itself . . . into a being in some measure self-conscious and free."[31] Reference to the creative activity of God is, in this view, a way of symbolizing the relationship of natural processes to the First Cause from which reality proceeds. Religious thinking differs from science in that it goes beyond the identification of material and efficient causes and speaks of an "ultimate" cause that gives reality an intrinsic goal, meaning, or purpose. It asks, what is it about the very nature of reality that allows natural selection to "edit" life in ways that have produced so much from so little? The process that has educed life from matter and mind from life is—for humans—the ultimate context of experience and is deservedly symbolized by the concept of God.

One helpful example of how religious thought might fashion an "existential response" to the ongoing creation of life on this planet is the theological efforts of the French priest and paleontologist Pierre Teilhard de Chardin.[32] In Teilhard's mystical reading of evolution, God was initially present in the universe as an eternal, self-sufficient First Being. Yet, God's creative powers made it imperative to "go out" from this original self-sufficiency into the "divine life" of ongoing or evolutionary creation. The initial pulse of creation was the act of dispersion whereby the First Being ("the One") gave rise to a vast multiplicity of universal matter ("the many"). The "divine life" refers to God's ongoing involvement in the evolutionary process. In this view the gradual convergence of life toward forms of increasing complexity and consciousness manifests the creative aims of the First Being. In this perspective evolution can be viewed as the process whereby "the many" have developed in ways that permit ever-greater capacities for individual organisms to express the life and creativity intrinsic to the original One. Although many of the biological conceptions Teilhard used to advance his theory have long since been refuted, his basic metatheoretical notion of a melioristic cosmos in which evolution carries forward God's creative aims is independent of specific scientific models and remains one of the most important religious syntheses of our era. As John Barrow and Frank Tipler note in *The Anthropic Cosmological Principle,* "the basic framework of [Teilhard's] theory is really the only framework wherein the evolving claims of modern science can be combined with an ultimate meaningfulness to reality."[33] Thus although it stands in need of considerable biological revision, Teilhard's model of God's presence in the evolutionary process nonetheless embodies precisely the kind of panpsychic vision needed to help modern Americans appreciate the ultimate context of human experience and to rededicate their desire to "serve God" by caring for the various orders of life.

The panpsychic aspect of James's "pluralistic panpsychism" accentuates our fundamental relatedness to the divine life. It holds out a vision of the inner availability of God's spiritual presence and thereby evokes an "aesthetic" existential response whereby we awaken to the imminent possibility of living in harmony with the divinity that flows through all things. Yet, it is the emphasis upon metaphysical pluralism that enabled James to show the spiritual significance of strenuous and caring moral action. James observed that the "ideal power with which we feel ourselves in connection" in mystical and religious experiences is ordinarily endowed with metaphysical attributes such as omnipotence and infinitude. Yet, in the interests of moral and intellectual clarity, this is probably an unwarranted extrapolation from the actual contents of religious experience. The only thing to which such experiences unequivocally testify is that we can experience union with something that is ontologically or cosmologically greater than ourselves and that in this union we find our greatest peace and fulfillment.[34] All that the facts obtained in radical empiricism require is that this "more" be other and cosmologically greater than our conscious selves. It is fully possible, and in fact much more consistent with practical reason, if this "more" be understood as finite and limited in knowledge or power, or both. In contrast to monism or conventional monotheism, in which God is understood as the sole sovereign power affecting the outcome of history, a pluralistic panpsychism detects divine spirit as "but one helper, primus inter pares, in the midst of all the shapers of the great world-fate."[35] God is thus to be thought of as an active force, but not the only force, in our evolving universe. The import of this view James summarized in this way:

87

> We are indeed internal parts of God and not external creation, on
> any possible reading of the panpsychic system. Yet because God is
> not the absolute, but is himself a part when the system is conceived
> pluralistically . . . the *salvation of the world [is] conditional* upon the
> success with which each unit does its part (emphasis added)."[36]

In a pluralistic universe, it is we who have the responsibility to carry the
life process forward. Real gains and real losses are at stake in the way we
conduct ourselves and shape the outcome of this unfinished universe.
Pluralism not only supports the strenuous mood, it demands it. It depicts
the world's salvation or its achievement of harmony as dependent upon the
energizing of its several parts, among which we are. It is by opening
ourselves to the creative influence of an immanent divine force that our
deepest destiny is fulfilled. The ultimate or intrinsic meaning of our lives is
to be found in assuming our role as codirectors of this melioristic universe.
Religious thought, then, must help induce the appropriate existential and
ethical response from the aesthetic perception that "we inhabit an invisible
spiritual environment from which help comes, our soul being mysteriously
one with a larger soul whose instruments we are."[37]

God and the Overcoming of Moral Blindness

As we have seen, our conceptions of God and of the ontological
structures that shape life are closely linked with our moral sensibilities. In
particular, they are capable of creating psychological structures that can
help us to overcome what James called the problem of "moral blindness."
Much of modern carelessness is due to the existence of psychological
barriers that wall us off from true reciprocity and empathic communication with others. These barriers cannot be commanded down. We cannot
produce genuine sensitivity to the needs and interests of others by a simple
act of will. The ability to care for causes beyond one's own immediate
gratification is grounded in the psychological capacity for "other-
regarding." This inner disposition toward perceiving and appreciating
others in their own right is a delicate psychological achievement. It
requires that we possess the sense of being a prized and cohesive self
(therefore creating less need to be self-centered). Genuine "other-
regarding" behavior also requires that we feel intimately connected with
life outside ourselves.

In the early part of chapter 2 we saw that humans have a need for the
continuous availability of a parent or idealized cultural object from which
they will receive a sense of meaningfulness and worth. The ability to feel

intimately united with some "higher reality" is important for the formation of an adequate sense of self-worth. And, too, the sense of relatedness to some "higher reality" (such as the parent in early childhood or God in later life) forms a psychological bridge whereby individuals gain a felt-sense of being related to the world outside themselves. Unfortunately, many people living in modern Western societies have at some point in the course of their development been psychologically affected by the absence of such experiences of merger with a "higher reality"—either in terms of improper parenting or the absence of a felt-sense of God, or both.[38]

The failure to have continuous access to a valued or idealized "other" thwarts the optimal development of a mature sense of self-esteem and fates individuals to the psychological condition of narcissism. In stark contrast to popular misconceptions of narcissism as a condition marked by excessive self-love, it is now understood to be the psychological consequence of an individual's inability to form relationships that provide recognition and a sense of self-worth. In other words, narcissism is characterized by too little, not too much, self-esteem. The core of the narcissistic condition is the formation of psychological barriers to protect the self from further emotional hurt. The individual becomes increasingly incapable of genuine reciprocity in relationships with others. Psychological narcissism is thus characterized by a shallow emotional life and almost total lack of empathy. The narcissistic personality is incapable of other-regarding behaviors such as intimacy or openness with others. He or she is closed off from the give and take of interpersonal relationships and consequently unable to recognize the needs of others or to identify with any consistent set of moral values. In short, he or she is psychologically incapable of escaping the moral blindness so prevalent in modern Western culture.

The psychoanalytic theorist Heinz Kohut has done much to show us that what we commonly call narcissism is only a pathological distortion of an otherwise healthy psychological condition. Kohut has emphasized that the "narcissistic need" to see ourselves mirrored and esteemed by the nurturing parent is in fact an indispensable part of full psychological health. The felt-sense of connectedness to a "higher reality" contributes to the development of a cohesive self and, in turn, to the ability to view others in their own right. A fundamental sense of feeling prized or worthy provides the foundation for the highest developmental achievements of adult life. Creativity, humor, empathy, genuine object love, and wisdom all require the capacity to engage life in ways that allow a felt-sense of continuity with the world. Thus, *if* our narcissistic needs are adequately met and channeled, they provide the foundation for the most mature and fulfilling engagements with life based upon what Kohut described as a "sense of supraindividual participation in the world."[39]

The heritage of aesthetic spirituality as depicted by such preeminent American writers as Emerson and James understands the religious resolution of this "certain blindness" so deeply rooted in our psychological nature. James was well aware of the intimate connection between religious experience and full psychological health. He argued, furthermore, that the experiential beauty of beholding an immanent divinity meets our fundamental need for relatedness with a higher reality even as it establishes a sense of continuity with the surrounding environment. James maintained that the most complete form of self-integration follows upon the person's discovery "that the tenderer parts of his personal life are continuous with a *more* of the same quality which is operative in the universe outside of him and which he can keep in working touch with."[40] An aesthetic spirituality makes the world over in ways that the rational intellect never can. It opens up a new perspective in which we can see ourselves as fundamentally connected with a wider universe that is itself fraught with an inner spiritual significance. The discovery of a point of inner continuity with the deeper reaches of existence "changes the dead blank *it* of the world into a living *thou,* with whom the whole man may have dealings."[41]

In this way James drew our attention to the need for a religious resolution to the psychological dilemma underlying so much of modern carelessness. The certain blindness in modern humans is caused not so much by the failure of proper authorities to command or coerce moral behavior but by the precariousness of our psychological natures. It is, finally, our inability to feel continuous with valued others or with a "higher" reality that renders the self too vulnerable, too unloved, too in need of constructing defensive barriers to be genuinely open to the needs and interests of others. Such barriers cannot be ordered down by rational appeals. They can, however, be made gradually more permeable as the self finds itself intimately and fundamentally related to the "more" of physical existence. The fundamental spiritual issue of our day, then, is that of making God accessible to the self. This is especially difficult for those for whom scriptures, rituals, and creeds no longer mediate such a vital sense of the "availability" of a higher, spiritual presence. It is imperative that religious thought, as well as religious practices such as meditation and sacraments, sensitize us to the imminent possibility of beholding a divine presence within and amidst human experience.

Salvation, Care, and the Divine Life

The style of religious thinking presented in this book calls for a shift in our conceptualization of God from imagery concerning a divine king to that of an orderly, innovating principle undergirding the evolutionary flux. This shift carries with it a change in the way we must understand other religious concepts such as sin and salvation. In biblical times sin was thought of as an act of personal disobedience. Sin represented personal estrangement from the commands of the divine king (or Father). It was consequently understood that each of us stands in personal need of receiving forgiveness from this divine king (or Father). Salvation has traditionally been understood as the reward and blessing that accompanies such forgiveness from a stern, but loving, Father-king. In this view, salvation is fundamentally an act of God's forgiveness. It represents an act of divine love in reconciling His creation back to Himself and making His creatures' eternal life possible despite their shortcomings and continuing errors.

The biblical views of sin and salvation stem from a mythic conception of God that can no longer be considered a metatheoretical understanding of the ultimate conditions that account for existence. Contemporary science renders such imagery of a God to whom we must relate as loyal subjects or guilt-ridden children obsolete. We now understand human existence in quite different terms. We know that human existence has emerged from a long and complex evolutionary history and that our existence is dependent upon the larger biological ecosystem that sustains life on this planet. In other words, we now know that our relationship to God's creative activity is mediated by our actions within the natural universe. This new view of our role in the divine life necessarily alters our understanding of what we must do to live in accordance with God's creative purpose. For example, Kaufman has suggested that sin "is not estrangement from God, as understood in such highly personalistic terms, but rather the steady undermining of the conditions that make meaningful and fruitful human life possible, through our pollution and poisoning of the ecosystem, on the one hand, and through social and political and economic arrangements that are oppressive and dehumanizing on the other."[42]

Salvation represents the personal and collective fulfillment that comes from participating in God's creative and unifying activity. We and God "have business" with one another, and our personal wholeness and fulfillment come through actively participating in those biological, psychological, sociological, economic, and political arrangements that foster the divine life. Thus, instead of understanding salvation as an isolated experience of relief from guilt, we must depict our ultimate fulfillment in terms of a progressive response to the lure of God's creative aims.[43]

The concept of salvation symbolizes a very particular interpretation of human wholeness. Although the concept of salvation affirms that wholeness includes adequate functioning within the natural and social orders, it adds the notion that in the final analysis human wholeness requires aligning our thoughts and actions with the "more" of empirical reality. Salvation pertains to the wholeness making that derives from participating in the divine life. Such participation consists, in part, in our own personal growth and the actualization of our potentials for expressing life. Each individual's self-development adds something new to existence and thereby enhances life's inner urge to increase the range of satisfaction and enrichment.[44]

Yet, as we discovered in chapter 2, the ultimate context of personal wholeness has to do with our ability to affirm that our lives have strengthened the sequence of generations and, in so doing, have participated in something of intrinsic meaning. Considered in terms of both the biological and the human ecosystems, life has an interdependent structure. Wholeness or fulfillment is thus necessarily a collective rather than a personal issue. In the complex web of life, individuality is important, but never final. An empirical understanding of the divine life makes it impossible to understand individual destiny independent of the larger creative effort in which God is involved. As Gordon Kaufman contends, "Life itself has a structure of interdependence, and unless human living and thinking and working can become increasingly oriented accordingly, and we learn to subordinate our particular interests and desires as individuals and communities, as religious and value traditions, as social classes and nation-states, to this wider loyalty to on-going life—both human and other—we shall certainly all perish."[45]

In this respect both the psychological development of the individual human and the long-term development of the human species testify to the fact that egocentrism (or kin favoring) stunts ongoing development. Both natural selection and the contingencies of behavioral reinforcement occasionally "favor" opportunistic and shortsighted forms of behavior. But "high adaptedness" does not always create high adaptability. This is particularly true when shortsighted behavior actually undermines or depletes the availability of resources that will be needed in the future. Human selfishness is a prime example of behavior that, although it appears to represent a developed capacity for agency, undermines our capacity for mutuality and makes it increasingly difficult to maintain fulfillment as we go through life. Erikson's emphasis upon "mutual activation" highlights precisely this principle that, in the long run, we gain in subjective enrichment only to the extent that we seek to occasion such enrichment in others.

The evolutionary biologist Theodosius Dobzhansky was enamored of Teilhard de Chardin's religious vision precisely because it brought this truth home so clearly. Following Teilhard, Dobzhansky asserts that "self-assertion which makes an individual break away from humanity is inimical to the growth of the person as well as of humanity. Healthy growth is fostered by love and arrested or stunted by egocentrism or egoism. Self-fulfillment is possible only through love for, and in a spiritual union with others. 'The true ego grows in inverse proportion to egoism.' "[46] Teilhard applied a similar logic to our understanding of the ongoing process of unification, convergence, and spiritualization of our planet. He was convinced that "no evolutionary future awaits man except in association with other men."[47] The point here is that we are not passive witnesses to evolution, but participants in the process who will direct its final outcome. Teilhard understands that our vision of the final "kingdom of God on earth" necessarily shapes our ethical commitments and thus needs to take seriously the fact that the web of life on this planet is bound together in the divine life.

> The consummation of the World, the gates of the Future, the entrance into the Superhuman, they do not open either to a few privileged or to one chosen people among all peoples! They will admit only an advance of all together, in a direction in which all together could join and achieve fulfillment in a spiritual renovation of the Earth."[48]

An evolving universe is a melioristic one. Its ultimate wholeness or salvation is neither necessary nor impossible. The "spiritual renovation of the Earth" is a possibility that becomes ever more a probability as the actual conditions of such renovation are established through human agency. To cease being a passive witness of evolution and instead to become an active participant means to care that these "actual conditions" are put into place. Becoming an instrument of the divine life entails conscientious concern to adjust our thought and action in ways commensurate with the larger scope of the evolutionary process. Doing "business with God" means ordering human life—including its institutions and customs and social practices, as well as its interpersonal dimension—in accord with our ultimate existential orientation to life.[49] We participate in the divine life not by offering praise to a Supreme Being during a weekly worship service, but by strenuously organizing the biological, social, economic, and political realms of human behavior in ways that permit the fullest expression and extension of life. Some social institutions, some economic structures, and some political agendas serve the divine life more than others. Participation in this ultimate orientation of life thereby requires strenuous efforts to understand and continually revise our commitments accordingly.

Jeffrey Wicken has poignantly underscored our ultimate responsibility for strenuous participation in the divine life by writing that evolution has moved from the blind and necessary to the seeing and volitional. It has been an opening up of possibility, and of conscious exploration of that possibility. The human responsibility is to continue this process of conscious manifestation—not just for our children or for any specific others, but for possibility in the ongoing process of Creation whose torch we carry.[50]

We can return now, one last time, to our question, Who cares? The person who cares is one who responds to the lure of the divine life and extends his or her identity to include a commitment to contribute to those conditions necessary for the spiritual renovation of the earth. Care emerges as a distinguishing characteristic of those persons who possess an aesthetic sensibility for the ultimate context of human experience. Caring is the existential and ethical response that is born of, and sustains our participation in, "the divinity that flows through all things."

Conclusion: Care, Commitment,

and the Cure of Souls

*

MODERN CARELESSNESS has its roots in social and cultural forces that warrant critical appraisal. We noted in the first chapter how the evolution peculiar to the human species is one that has shifted from genes to memes. That is, humanity's relatively large cerebral cortex "loosens" the otherwise fixed wiring of genetic influences upon behavior. Human behavior is largely under the controlling influence of the socialization process and accumulated cultural knowledge (memes). It is reasonable to ask just how and why contemporary American society promotes the quest for individual gratification while doing so little to reinforce the claims of community. It is also reasonable to ask which cultural institutions appear most capable of remedying modern carelessness and of giving rise to a new and more ecologically sensitive American character.

Culture, Religion, and Adaptation

Humans are born incomplete or unfinished animals. What sets us apart from other species is our sheer capacity to learn and to complete ourselves through the knowledge provided to us by our surrounding culture. The human brain and human culture evolved in a complex, interactive way. A cybernetic or feedback system developed whereby the brain and culture continued to shape one another's evolutionary progress. Without culture, human behavior would be too random and too anarchic to permit survival. Culture provides an extrasomatic source of information that completes human nature even as it molds it in ways that foster group cohesion and adaptation. In this sense, culture is an evolutionary-adaptive mechanism that serves to govern individuals' behavior in ways that function in service of the group. The customs, taboos, rituals, and

95

knowledge transmitted by culture have been "selected for" in evolutionary history insofar as they have served the overall purpose of group adaptation.

The "sources of information" supplied by culture (memes) can be likened to a blueprint or template that provides a prepared pattern for human behavior. The cultural anthropologist Clifford Geertz discerned that the symbolic forms of culture provide "the link between what men are intrinsically capable of becoming and what they actually, one by one, in fact become."[1] By submitting to the symbolically mediated forms through which culture directs us to express ideas, create tools, and organize social behavior, the human race has gradually shaped its own destiny. Our memes construct a world and, in turn, create new directions for our own individual and collective development. That we create memes is a necessity of our evolutionary-adaptive makeup. Yet, the specific memes we create and disseminate are products of social and historical chance and should, furthermore, be continuously subjected to philosophical reflection. For just as all genetic mutations are surely not adaptive in the long run, so are cultural memes but mutations that have differing probabilities of guiding the human species in enriching ways.

Throughout world history religion has functioned as a principal source of the memes that govern individual attitudes and behaviors. Religion is the primary means through which civilizations conserve the fund of general meanings in terms of which people interpret or organize their experience. It was in this context that Geertz formulated the classic anthropological definition of religion as "(1) a system of symbols which acts to (2) establish powerful, pervasive, and long-lasting moods and motivations in men by (3) formulating conceptions of a general order of existence and (4) clothing these conceptions with such an aura of factuality that (5) the moods and motivations seem uniquely realistic."[2] Geertz's point here is that it is an empirical fact that religion has emerged and functions in human society in ways that incorporate individuals into a shared way of life. Religion is, in this sense, among the most crucial adaptive activities of the human species. It puts an interpretative or evaluative "map" upon our psychological tendencies that directs us to meaningful and socially fulfilling action. In fulfilling this evolutionary-adaptive need of the human species, Geertz writes, "the religious perspective differs from the common-sensical in that, as already pointed out, it moves *beyond* the realities of everyday life *to wider ones* which *correct and complete* them."[3]

It is this last element of religion's unique capacity for engendering a "cultural system"—its ability to identify wider realities that correct and complete everyday life—that makes it so important to our interdisciplinary analysis of care. An empirically based study of care must be prepared to examine cultural systems in terms of how fully they widen the scope of human concern, how deeply they invoke human commitment, and how effectively they foster meaningful and productive human actions. The concluding portions of this book will attempt to open up a discussion of the role that religion and religious professionals might perform in counteracting the carelessness of modern society and establishing instead a culture that more carefully locates individuals within the larger web of life on this planet.

Modern Social Structure and the Crisis of Commitment

Modern American society has developed out of a historical matrix that at least potentially supports a conscientious or strenuous stance toward life. The two major intellectual traditions from which American culture emerged were the rationalistic ethos spawned by Enlightenment intellectuals such as Thomas Jefferson and Benjamin Franklin and the Judeo-Christian biblical heritage brought to the New World by any number of denominational groups. Both cultural traditions originally contained conceptual and institutional resources for balancing a strong emphasis upon individualism with a clear recognition of the need for community. Even the Enlightenment rationalism of America's founders was predicated upon certain religious (deistic) principles that fostered personal commitment both to self-cultivation and to community building. Among these convictions of our nation's founders were belief in a creator god, emphasis upon moral virtue as the definitive characteristic of individual integrity, commitment to a work ethic that held that personal success and public respect will come to all who assert and discipline themselves, and faith that the laws of nature are divinely appointed mechanisms for moving history toward some ultimate destiny. The secular and sacred origins of Americans' world outlook fit together quite nicely and together fostered loyalty to the nation's democratically chosen purposes.

These two interconnected strands of American culture were imparted to individual character through the socializing mechanisms of a largely agrarian economy. The economic and social sanctions wrought by the interdependence of rural and small-town living shaped human relationships. Voluntary cooperation, mutual concern, and gregariousness were not just virtues but practical necessities. And although there were diverse ethnic and regional subcultures from the very outset, there was a sufficient degree of social and economic interdependence in early American life to forge commitment to a common set of values and meanings.

Unfortunately, both the Enlightenment rationalism and the Puritan-inspired religious faith of our nation's founders have lost the language and the socializing mechanisms to preserve the delicate balance between individualism and communal commitment.[4] The reasons for this are, at root, changes in American social structures and the continuing pluralization of the intellectual traditions competing for our personal and collective allegiance. As an agrarian economy gave way first to an industrial and gradually to a postindustrial economic base, the rules governing social interaction have changed imperceptibly. Spontaneous interaction and uncoerced cooperation have been replaced by unmitigating competition and calculated efforts to manipulate. Small-town living has given way to the anonymity of larger cities. Rapid movement between neighborhoods or even regions of the country has drastically diminished any obvious claims that communities might have upon individual citizens. No longer can peer opinion have the socializing power it formerly exercised. And, too, the massive scale of American economic and political life lulls individuals into passivity and complacency. Individual action—political or ecological—seems to count for less and less.

Relentless immigration has led to a more diversified and enriched American "meme pool." Yet the short-term consequence of this social pluralization has been an attendant pluralization in religious faiths, customs, and moral outlooks. Added to this, post-Darwinian science has combined with the relativizing impact of critical inquiries into the origins of the Bible in ways that have undermined intellectual certainty in religious "truth." All in all, a crisis has emerged in both moral and religious "justification"; what were once certain truths are now seen to be culturally conditioned and to rest on shaky historical and intellectual premises. Widespread skepticism—particularly among intellectuals and educators—about moral and religious beliefs further eroded the formation of a cultural system capable of imparting an adaptive orientation to life.

The greatest casualty of this pluralization in American social and intellectual life has been our decreasing ability to make meaningful commitments. By this I mean that our culture no longer imparts the resolve or discipline to pursue a consistently caring course of action. My point here connects with Erik Erikson's contention that a healthy identity presupposes the virtue of fidelity. Fidelity, for Erikson, is the ability to sustain commitments even when faced with temptations to "jump horses" and follow newly emerging opportunities. In Erikson's view, a stable sense of identity requires a consistent sense of orientation that comes from thoughtful adherence to a well-defined set of values or ideas. In my opinion, it is precisely the lack of such fidelity that is responsible for the failure of modern people to find enduring intimacy in interpersonal relationships or to become generative in their adult years. Genuine caring requires and presupposes this psychological capacity for fidelity and commitment.

Social and intellectual pluralization potentially bodes well for a culture in terms of adding greater diversity of the meme pool. As yet, however, no new synthesis has emerged in American life that is capable of forging consensus concerning shared values and meanings. Our cultural confusion has utterly undermined individuals' capacity for fidelity and commitment. Modern social structures foster a psychological preference for minimizing commitments and for remaining permanently tentative about what persons or causes are "worth" the investment of our time and energy. Since trustworthy values are not forthcoming from the outer or public sphere, individuals are forced back upon their own inner or private psychological resources. Philip Rieff has aptly characterized the type of personality most characteristic of our age as "psychological man."[5] The modern "psychological" personality differs markedly from the predominant character type of other historical and cultural eras. He or she does not share the same values as the "religious" person of our Hebrew and Christian heritage, the "political" person of our classical Greek and Roman heritage, or even the "economic" person formed by the early industrial era and the rationalist ideals of the Enlightenment. These previous cultural models embodied normative conceptions whereby individuals understood how they are fundamentally related to a larger (religious, civic, or socioeconomic) whole. And, too, the religious, political, and economic models of character all identified the requirements of a just society in ways that put distinct restraints upon the tendency toward individual gratification.

By contrast, the modern "psychological" person has not been socialized into any intact community of shared cultural norms. He or she has become sufficiently skeptical of the truth or merit of competing moral or religious systems as to be characterologically suspicious of any claim made upon his or her pursuit of personal fulfillment. The modern character, Rieff says, "is antiheroic, shrewd, carefully counting . . . satisfactions and dissatisfactions, studying unprofitable commitments as the sins most to be avoided."[6] In the pursuit of personal fulfillment, he or she makes a virtue of avoiding commitments, keeping all options open, remaining free from externally imposed restraints. In short, he or she is psychologically disposed against caring for anything that would put a burden upon short-term personal gratification. To the modern, psychologically sophisticated person, caring is simply not worth the personal cost.

An engaging commentary on Americans' inability to make meaningful commitments appeared in one of the best-selling novels of the 1970s, *Zen and the Art of Motorcycle Maintenance*. In it Robert Pirsig cleverly described motorcycle maintenance in such a way as to make it a metaphor for "the art of rationality itself." Pirsig's intention was to examine the attitudes that keep us and our relationships with the world around us in proper working condition. He observed, "Working on a motorcycle, working well, caring, is to become part of a process."[7] The process Pirsig had in mind was the process of the web of life, a process whose elements or parts are held together by care. His allusion to Zen was meant to convey his conviction that true care proceeds from an aesthetic or religious sense of personal connection with a deeper order of life. The "art" or rationality of care requires the cultivation of a felt-sense of this connectedness, a vivid sense of participating in life at a level in which there is an absence of subject-object duality and in which the divisions between "self" and "other" melt away. As Pirsig put it, when we are not dominated by feelings of separateness from our work, then and only then can we be said to 'care' about what we are doing. "That is what caring really is, a feeling of identification with what one's doing."[8]

Pirsig was well aware that care is more than a feeling. To really count for something tangible in our world, care must express itself in commitment. Strenuous care entails discipline and resolve. Pirsig called this "old-fashioned gumption." No amount of government-administered programs can begin to reorient our society unless they are "built on a foundation of [strenuous care] within the individuals involved. We've had that individual [strenuous care] in the past, exploited it as a natural resource without knowing it, and now it's just about depleted. Everyone's just about out of gumption. . . . We need a return to individual integrity, self-reliance and old-fashioned gumption."[9]

I am not really sure where we Americans will go to find a new supply of the gumption it takes to care for ourselves and our world. I am certain, however, that Pirsig and the "deep ecologists" are right in believing that it will require the emergence of a new cultural outlook predicated upon an aesthetic or religious rather than a strictly ethical view of the individual's place in the larger scheme of things. Modern people are too sophisticated in their pursuit of psychological fulfillment to rearrange their priorities solely on the basis of logical appeals to the well-being of future generations. Attitudes and behaviors that are genuinely other-regarding cannot be commanded by rational argument. But they can be induced through the kind of nonegoistic, Zen-like ways of viewing the world that Pirsig drew our attention to and that the proponents of American "aesthetic spirituality" have long championed as the key to mature self-reliance. Put differently, it is futile to tell modern "psychological" people that they shouldn't try to safeguard their individual satisfactions and seek to avoid unprofitable commitments.

We might better succeed in awakening gumption if we concentrate instead on helping people to broaden their sense of self in ways that demonstrate just how fully psychological fulfillment is rooted in the larger process of Being. In part, this can be accomplished through cognitive or educational means by exposing people to the broader vision of the interconnectedness of life depicted by the natural and social sciences. Awareness of the stubborn facts concerning the interdependence of all developmental processes (including our own) can surely lead to a widening sense of self and a widening sense of identification with the claims being made upon us from without. Yet, broadening our identity in ways that elicit care also requires a Zen-like aesthetic feel for the intrinsic value of activities transpiring within the web of life. The self that is most fully capable of care is one that is freed from a strictly egoistic, utilitarian mode of calculating satisfaction. The surest source of the stamina or gumption needed to sustain meaningful commitments flows from a religious sense of our connectedness to a spiritual "more." For this reason an essay on care must conclude with observations concerning how those entrusted with the engendering and maintaining of culture—those engaged in "cure of souls" in the largest sense of this term—might best contribute to what Pirsig described as "a return to individual integrity."

Commitment and the Cure of Souls

The task of guiding people toward healthy and meaningful life-styles is traditionally referred to as the "cure of souls." Every society in human history has given rise to institutions responsible for engendering cultural values and assisting its members to pattern their lives in accordance with these values. This task of cultural maintenance has taken many forms throughout the history of world civilization.[10] In ancient Greece, philosophers were "physicians of the soul" and wove theology, philosophy, and psychology into a comprehensive guide to the reasons for human suffering and the secret of a balanced life. In ancient Israel, the Jewish community looked to wise men, scribes, and rabbis for advice concerning how best to accord their lives with God's will for humanity. Hinduism and Buddhism have long relied on "holy men" of various kinds to serve as teachers or gurus for those seeking assistance along the path to enlightenment. Modern Westerners rely both on secular professionals—educators and psychotherapists—and on religious professionals—rabbis, priests, and ministers—for assisting people to live healthy, productive lives. It is to these professionals that we must direct our attention if we seek to sketch out some guidelines for reequipping Americans with the gumption to care strenuously for themselves and for the world they live in.

In their study of the range of activities associated with the cure of souls, William Clebsch and Charles Jaekle identified four separate activities performed by those who try to help others live healthy and meaningful lives.[11] The first of these activities is healing, including all of those activities necessary for helping people to achieve mental, emotional, and psychological health. The second activity is helping to sustain people in times of loss, which has to do with assisting them to attain perspectives upon life that identify possibilities for continued personal growth even amid life's hardships. The third activity associated with the cure of souls is offering moral guidance, and the fourth is helping to reestablish broken relationships between people and their fellow human beings as well as between people and God.

Our anthropology of care has clearly established that there is necessarily a religious dimension (broadly defined) to each of these four functions of cultural maintenance. The attainment of a certain spiritual orientation to life is, as Erikson's notions of trust and wisdom indicate, a prerequisite for full psychological health. My *Religion and the Life Cycle* depicts in greater detail the vast extent to which human fulfillment throughout the course of life depends upon values and experiences that have a distinctively religious character.[12] Thus the most complete form of psychological healing—whether offered by religious or secular professionals—must entail a broadly spiritual dimension. Our previous discussions of deep ecology, Kohlberg's notion of the highest stages of moral development, and James's astute observation concerning the intimate relationship between religious conviction and the strenuous mood similarly reveal the spiritual character of activities aimed at sustaining, guiding, or reestablishing broken relationships with other people, with the natural universe, or with the divine life.

For this reason I believe that the first steps toward the kind of cultural renewal required of our age must take a religious form. Even educators and therapists who work outside any overtly religious setting must nonetheless become more explicit about the broadly spiritual aspects of the care or guidance of human beings. Toward this end I think it important that all our "helping professions" become more sophisticated in conceptualizing the relationship of their therapeutic activities to those moral and spiritual norms rooted in the ecology of care. To be sure, various psychotherapists—particularly those working out of a Jungian orientation or various "third force" orientations—have sought to do this during the last few decades. And, too, many educators have tried to articulate certain clusters of values and moral considerations they feel are essential to the guidance of our young. Far more promising, however, has been the attempt of religious professionals to formulate a "practical theology" that depicts the goals and methods of the many forms of care undertaken by pastors and church congregations. Practical theology is entirely distinct from dogmatic or fundamental theology in that it is not concerned with explicating or defending specific doctrines or creeds. Whereas fundamental theology is a largely deductive activity concerned with a particular denomination's understanding of "theoretical reason," practical theology is more akin to the style of religious reflection outlined in chapter 4. It is concerned solely with offering care and direction to "practical reason" as individuals seek to adapt to life in ways that yield maximum enrichment to themselves, the wider community, and the divine life from which all being proceeds. Practical theology is therefore the intellectual and theoretical foundation for the practice of the cure of souls. Its task is to conceptualize the appropriate means of engaging in such varied practices as counseling or therapy, education aimed at meaningful living, and providing ritualized experiences that bring people into more complete harmony with themselves, their fellow human beings, and the divine life of creativity within the natural order.

Because the cure of souls is an activity that concerns itself with nurturing and guiding "practical reason," it can and must be a professional discipline that proceeds directly from knowledge accumulated by the natural and social sciences. In contrast to fundamental theology, which proceeds from revelations and traditions specific to a given religious heritage, the cure of souls is a religious function that must be informed by empirically based knowledge concerning the psychological and sociological determinants of behavior. What I have in mind as a method for "practical theology" is consistent with what is frequently referred to as the correlational model, first developed by Paul Tillich and subsequently refined by David Tracy and Don Browning.[13] Tillich sought to accommodate religious thinking to modern intellectual thought by maintaining that theology should proceed by correlating existential questions drawn from philosophical and scientific analyses of the human condition with the "answers" furnished by Christian doctrinal theology. Tracy and Browning, realizing that Tillich's method finally does not allow the human sciences to inform religious thought in any substantial way, propose a revised correlational method whereby the natural and social sciences can substantially contribute to the religious "answers" concerning the nature of human fulfillment.

I would push this correlational model a bit further and maintain that the practice of the cure of souls requires a theoretical model informed almost entirely by the insights from such empirical disciplines as evolutionary biology, sociobiology, sociology, and psychology. Collectively, these disciplines depict human needs, tendencies, and drives in ways that illuminate our efforts to enhance people's efforts to live, to live well, and to increase their range of satisfactions. Put differently, the human sciences provide publicly accessible discussions of the "good" (physical, social, and psychological fulfillment), which constitute the professional knowledge base for practitioners of the cure of souls. What practitioners of the cure of souls bring to this empirical knowledge base is a commitment to understanding the wider moral and religious "environments" to which people must also adapt themselves in their quests for wholeness and fulfillment. They understand that humans do not simply adapt themselves to a world that is already "out there" in some tangible way. Instead, humans also live in a world of meanings and values that must be created and maintained through commitment. Thus the cure of souls is an activity that is profoundly ecological in outlook and must assist people to pursue fulfillment in ways that simultaneously strengthen their connectedness with the wider community and the natural order.

The ecology of care makes it clear that those entrusted with the cure of souls are entrusted with more than simply alleviating emotional or motivational difficulties. They are also entrusted with helping to establish, maintain, and disseminate a cultural vision that will enable people to make meaningful commitments. Practitioners of the cure of souls must be mindful of the fact that humans can and must construct a symbolic world for themselves that will shape their overall outlook, values, and range of commitments. It is their task to be self-conscious about accepting this responsibility and to bring a consistently ethical orientation to their efforts aimed at healing, sustaining, guiding, and reconciling the lives of those whose care is entrusted to them. As Don Browning cautioned in his thoughtful *The Moral Context of Pastoral Care,* concern with healing and guiding persons "should never be understood simply as a matter of 'loosening people up,' helping them to become 'more open' or more 'spontaneous and flexible,' 'removing their guilt,' or making them 'more loving.' . . . [It] must first be concerned to give a person a structure, a character, an identity, a religiocultural value system out of which to live."[14] Religious congregations (and, for that matter, college campuses that take seriously their role as formative cultural agents) are prime examples of the type of social institution best able to provide people with such a "religiocultural value system." Such a task requires an intact community concerned with projecting thoughtful conceptions of humanity's long-term values or objectives while drawing attention to the tragic consequences of our tendency to indulge ourselves in immediate gratifications.

Practitioners of the cure of souls must also project a cultural vision that deepens each person's perceptions of the divine life, which ultimately empowers and bestows meaning upon the whole web of life. Overcoming moral blindness and adopting an attitude of care requires the sense of intrinsic value that comes only from a religious understanding of human fulfillment. Religious perspective in no way alters the substantive information concerning healthy human functioning that empirical disciplines bring to acts of healing, sustaining, guiding, and reconciling. A religious perspective does, however, provide an additional evaluative perspective based upon the conviction (faith) that the most complete form of human adaptation requires that we also adapt ourselves to the "more" of physical existence. Thus, although the cure of souls adduces no unique information of its own on issues of psychological health or therapeutic technique, it does order such information according to certain evaluative criteria inherent in its concern with the widest possible environment to which humans ought to adapt themselves. Thus, for example, religious perspective attests to the interconnectedness of the universe and to the intrinsic value of each and every being within the web of life, not as simple sentiments but rather as metaphysical facts that warrant our awe-inspired reverence. And, too, religious perspective provides a vivid sense of the essentially melioristic character of life (viewed as an expression of the divine life) and in so doing shows that we have not just a moral but also an ontological obligation to participate in melioristic or wholeness-producing activities of all kinds.

I would, furthermore, suggest that religious perspective reshapes empirical information concerning human fulfillment by offering a distinctive interpretation of the who, what, and how of human existence. By this I mean that a religious perspective opens us to a different perspective of our identity (the "who"), our final reason or goal for living (the "what"), and the techniques or strategies through which we best express this reason or achieve this goal (the "how"). The cure of souls consequently calls us to view life with a different witness and to respond to life with a different voice. First, and perhaps foremost, is the different conception of personal identity that practical theology insists must undergird all activities of counseling, education, and community formation. Practical theology locates all psychological information concerning the formation of the self in terms of "the ultimate context" of existence. That is, it views the developing self from the perspective of creative aims of the divine life (being created in the image of God). Religious conviction—Jewish, Christian, Muslim, or Hindu—orients us to the distinctive affirmation that we are not bodies who possibly possess a spirit or soul, but rather that we are spirits or souls that are expressing the divine life of creation through physical bodies. The different voice born of religious perspective understands sociobiological, sociological, and psychological accounts of personal identity as important accounts of the material and efficient causes shaping our lives. It insists, however, that the final or ultimate cause of existence is the divine life in terms of which we must finally identify ourselves.

In chapter 4 we defined the essential task of religious thought as that of orienting people to the broadest range of experience, describing what experience testifies to be its ultimate context, and of inducing the appropriate existential and ethical response. It follows, then, that when "practical theology" seeks to identify the reason or goal of life, it speaks in a different voice than do those perspectives that emphasize social, economic, or political activity. The different voice of religious conviction draws our attention to the myriad ways in which our individual lives participate in the ultimate aims of the divine life. Our individual quests for the ongoing enrichment of life can be affirmed as furthering the melioristic creativity of being itself. In this sense the developmental challenges confronting us throughout life can be affirmed as opportunities for spiritual growth. Every role, relationship, responsibility, and vocational task can be religiously interpreted as opportunities to respond to the divine lure of creativity. This different voice simultaneously affirms that our ultimate worth as humans is never at the mercy of outer circumstances. No event, no loss—no matter how brutal or unjust—can rob us of our capacity to develop charity, patience, understanding, resilience, or courage. Religiously interpreted, it is not so much events themselves that affect whether we accomplish our ultimate goal in life as it is the attitude we take toward these events. The appropriate existential response that we are called upon to make is to be ever perceptive of new opportunities to respond to life in creative, melioristic ways. We can maximize our spiritual growth by sustained commitment to participating in the divine life of care.

Proclaiming that our ultimate reason for living is to participate in the divine life of creation, the religious perspective not surprisingly directs our attention to a very different set of adaptive activities. Most importantly, it illuminates the value of inwardness and receptivity. Practical theology predicates all of its activities of care on the reality of the divine life. Consequently, its practice of healing, guidance, or reconciliation of broken relationships must emphasize techniques aimed at fostering an aesthetic appreciation of this spiritual presence. The cure of souls must necessarily entail such activities as meditation and ritual, insofar as these activities can awaken in us an appreciation of our intimate connection with what Emerson described as "the divinity that flows through all things." Thus, unlike contemporary self-help manuals that extol such techniques as networking or systematic manipulation of others' vulnerabilities, the cure of souls directs us to periods of quiet, of seeking receptivity to the "more" of personal life, and of becoming sufficiently empty of egocentric concerns that we might better hear and respond to the needs of those about us.

The cure of souls, then, is a cultural institution capable of rekindling old-fashioned commitment both to self-cultivation and to the building of cohesive communities. By illuminating what experience shows to be the ultimate context of our individual quests for identity (who), purpose (what), and effective adaptive strategies (how), those entrusted with the tasks of healing and guidance might effectively elicit the existential and ethical response of strenuous care. Educators, therapists, and especially those religious professionals involved in pastoral care have the responsibility for the creation and maintenance of a culture attentive to the psychological prerequisites of care. The self that is truly capable of lasting commitments is one who has a vivid sense of continuity with a spiritual "more" from which our ultimate identity and purpose is derived. In this way we become freed from a strictly egoistic, utilitarian mode of calculating satisfaction and instead come to view service to the wider web of life as a personal virtue rather than a sin to be avoided. In short, those professions with the educational and ritualistic resources for evoking a religious perspective of our natural order would seem to be the surest source of the spiritual stamina needed to fuel old-fashioned gumption and to make meaningful commitments possible.

Notes

✳

Introduction:
Who Cares?

1. Ernest Boyer, *College: The Undergraduate Experience in America* (New York: Harper & Row, 1987), p. 99.

2. Ibid. Boyer observes that university education has over time become captive to the economic and cultural forces that feed this call to individual gratification. Emphasis upon vocational education and preparing young men and women for postgraduation employment has eroded the ability of universities to help students gain a wider perspective upon themselves and their world.

3. My use of the term "limit dimension" comes from David Tracy's *Blessed Rage for Order* (New York: Seabury Press, 1975), in which he argues that modern religious thought should build upon analyses of those experiences that reveal the limit dimension to human experience. According to Tracy, the limit dimension of human experience is revealed in those situations in which people find themselves confronted with an ultimate limit or horizon, situations that force us to acknowledge the limits or limitations of a strictly rational approach to life. I have shown how this concept helps construct a religious interpretation of human psychological development in my *Religion and the Life Cycle* (Philadelphia: Fortress Press, 1988).

Chapter 1
Evolution, Adaptation, and Care

1. Numerous books can serve as general introductions to evolutionary science. *Evolution* (San Francisco: W. H. Freeman & Co., 1977), coauthored by Theodosius Dobzhansky, Francisco Ayala, G. Ledyard Stebbins, and James Valentine, is particularly helpful. Colin Patterson's *Evolution* (Ithaca, N.Y.: Cornell University Press, 1978) is a little old, perhaps, but still a useful introduction to the field. George Gaylord Simpson's *The Meaning of Evolution* (New Haven, Conn.: Yale University Press, 1949) resulted from the Terry Lectures that Simpson delivered on "a study of

the history of life and of its significance for man." Douglas J. Futuyama's *Science on Trial: The Case for Evolution* (New York: Pantheon Press, 1983) is a spirited and partisan defense of Darwinism as over and against the antievolutionary position that often goes under the name "creation science." Antony Flew's *Darwinian Evolution* (London: Granada Publications, 1984) provides a thoughtful philosophical analysis and support of Darwin's major theses. The more advanced reader might also wish to consult Ernst Mayr's *Evolution and the Diversity of Life* (Cambridge, Mass.: Belknap Press, 1976), G. Ledyard Stebbins, *Darwin to DNA, Molecules to Humanity* (San Francisco: W. H. Freeman & Company, 1982), and E. Sober, ed., *Conceptual Issues in Evolutionary Biology* (Cambridge, Mass.: MIT Press, 1984).

2. Simpson, *Meaning of Evolution*, p. 281.

3. Charles Darwin, *The Origin of Species* (New York: Mentor Books, 1958), p. 74.

4. Dobzhansky et al., *Evolution*, p. 66.

5. Darwin, cited in Dobzhansky et al., *Evolution*, p. 97.

6. Darwin, cited in Futuyama, *Science on Trial*, p. 34.

7. Ibid.

8. Dobzhansky et al., *Evolution*, p. 31.

9. Simpson, *Meaning of Evolution*, p. 198.

10. Ibid.

11. Futuyama, *Science on Trial*, p. 131.

12. Simpson, *Meaning of Evolution*, p. 261.

13. Dobzhansky et al., *Evolution*, p. 503. Ernst Mayr, in his *Evolution and the Diversity of Life*, provides a succinct explanation of the apparent "design" in nature.

> The product of selection is adaptation and the adaptedness of organisms and their utilization of the environment is improved from generation to generation until it appears as perfect as if it was the product of design. In short, the solution of Darwin's paradox is that natural selection itself turns accident into design. (p. 43)

14. Simpson, *Meaning of Evolution*, p. 262.

15. See G. Ledyard Stebbins, *The Basis of Progressive Evolution* (Chapel Hill, N.C.: University of North Carolina Press, 1969).

16. See Francisco Ayala, "The Concept of Biological Progress," in Francisco Ayala and Theodosius Dobzhansky, eds., *Studies in the Philosophy of Biology* (London: Macmillan Publishers, 1974).

17. Patterson, *Evolution*, p. 178.

18. Konrad Lorenz, *On Aggression* (New York: Harcourt, Brace & World, 1963), p. 265.

19. Edward O. Wilson, *Sociobiology: The New Synthesis* (Cambridge, Mass.: Belknap Press, 1975), p. 550.

20. Simpson, *Meaning of Evolution*, p. 287.

21. William James, "Remarks on Spencer's Definition of Mind as Correspondence," in *Collected Essays and Reviews* (New York: Longmans, Green & Co., 1920), p. 52.

22. William James, "Great Men in Their Environment," in *The Will to Believe* (New York: Dover Publications, 1956), p. 218.

23. Ibid.

24. Michael Ruse, "Darwinism and Determinism," *Zygon* 22 (Dec., 1987): 422.

25. Dobzhansky et al., *Evolution*, p. 455.

26. Simpson, *Meaning of Evolution*, p. 287.

27. Patterson, *Evolution*, p. 178.

28. Julian Huxley, *Evolution in Action* (New York: Harper & Brothers, 1953), p. 132.

29. The field of sociobiology is rife with spirited debate. The classic text in the field is Edward O. Wilson's *Sociobiology*. Arthur L. Caplan's edited volume *The Sociobiology Debate* (New York: Harper & Row, 1978) contains forty-two articles that examine the problems and promises of sociobiological explanations of human behavior. Readers might also wish to consult G. Stent's edited volume *Morality as a Biological Phenomenon: The Presuppositions of Sociobiological Research* (Berkeley, Calif.: University of California Press, 1980) and Ashley Montagu, ed., *Sociobiology Examined* (New York: Oxford University Press, 1980). Helpful critiques of sociobiology are found in P. Kitcher's *Vaulting Ambition: Sociobiology and the Quest for Human Nature* (Cambridge, Mass.: MIT Press, 1985) and Michael Ruse, *Sociobiology: Sense or Nonsense?* (Boston: D. Reidel, 1979).

30. Wilson, *Sociobiology*, p. 3.

31. The term "kin selection" is generally attributed to W. D. Hamilton in his "The Genetical Evolution of Social Behaviour," *Journal of Theoretical Biology* 7 (1964): 1–52. Earlier studies demonstrating the extent to which relatives benefit from a person's altruistic behavior were conducted by geneticists J. B. S. Haldane and R. A. Fisher.

32. The concept of "reciprocal altruism" received its major formulation in R. L. Trivers, "The Evolution of Reciprocal Altruism," *Quarterly Review of Biology* 46 (1971): 35–57.

33. Ruse, "Darwinism and Determinism," p. 425.

34. Charles Darwin, *The Descent of Man*, ch. 4, p. 498, cited in Jeffrie Murphy, *Evolution, Morality, and the Meaning of Life* (Totowa, N.J.: Rowman & Littlefield, 1982), p. 73.

35. Murphy, *Evolution, Morality, and Meaning*, p. 73.

36. Darwin, *Descent of Man*, ch. 5, p. 500, and ch. 21, p. 914, cited in Murphy, *Evolution, Morality, and Meaning*, p. 78.

37. Dobzhansky et al., *Evolution*, p. 457.

38. For a discussion of the role that Darwin attributed to reason in humanity's moral life, see Murphy, *Evolution, Morality, and Meaning*, p. 78.

39. Wilson, *Sociobiology*, p. 562.

40. Edward O. Wilson, *On Human Nature* (Cambridge, Mass.: Harvard University Press, 1978), pp. 547–575.

41. My position here is similar to the argument made by Thomas B. Colwell,

Jr., when he wrote that "the balance of Nature provides an objective normative model which can be utilized as the ground of human value. . . . Nor does the balance of Nature serve as the source of all our values. It is only the *ground* of whatever other values we may develop. But these other values must be consistent with it. . . . The ends which we propose must be such as to be compatible with it." See his article "The Balance of Nature: A Ground for Human Values" in *Main Currents in Modern Thought* 26 (Dec., 1969), p. 50.

42. The entire last section of this chapter borrows heavily from the excellent overview of environmental science in G. Tyler Miller, *Environmental Science* (Belmont, Calif.: Wadsworth Publishing Co., 1988).

43. Ibid., p. 18.

44. Aldo Leopold, *A Sand County Almanac* (New York: Oxford University Press, 1966), p. 219.

45. See Bill Devall and George Sessions, *Deep Ecology* (Salt Lake City: Peregrine Smith Books, 1985).

46. Dobzhansky et al., *Evolution*, p. 473.

47. George Gaylord Simpson, *This View of Life* (New York: Harcourt, Brace & World, 1964), p. 105.

Chapter 2
The Self

1. David Bakan, *The Duality of Human Existence* (Chicago: Rand McNally & Co., 1966). I might here acknowledge that this paragraph follows closely a line of reasoning argued cogently in a chapter titled "Culture, Religion, and Care" in Don Browning's excellent (though too narrowly titled) book *The Moral Context of Pastoral Care* (Philadelphia: Westminster Press, 1976).

2. Andras Angyal, *Foundations for a Science of Personality* (New York: Oxford University Press, 1941).

3. Andras Angyal, "A Theoretical Model for Personality Studies," in Clark E. Moustakas, ed., *The Self* (New York: Harper & Row, 1956), p. 45.

4. Arthur Deikman, "Bimodal Consciousness," *Archives of General Psychiatry* 225 (Dec., 1971): 481–489.

5. Robert Ornstein, *The Psychology of Consciousness* (New York: Viking Press, 1972), p. 52.

6. Erik Erikson, *Insight and Responsibility* (New York: W. W. Norton & Co., 1967), p. 165.

7. Erik Erikson, *Childhood and Society* (New York: W. W. Norton & Co., 1963), p. 263.

8. Erik Erikson, *Identity, Youth, and Crisis* (New York: W. W. Norton & Co., 1968), p. 138.

9. Erikson, *Insight and Responsibility*, p. 130.

10. Ibid., p. 131.

11. Ibid.

12. The interested reader can find helpful discussions of adult developmental stages in Bernice Neugarten's *Middle Age and Aging* (Chicago: University of Chicago Press, 1968) and Erik Erikson, ed., *Adulthood* (New York: W. W. Norton & Co., 1978).

13. Daniel Levinson, *The Seasons of a Man's Life* (New York: Alfred A. Knopf, 1978).

14. See Carol Gilligan, *In a Different Voice: Psychological Theory and Women's Development* (Cambridge, Mass.: Harvard University Press, 1982).

15. Lawrence Kohlberg, "Continuities and Discontinuities in Childhood and Adult Moral Development Revisited" in R. Baltes and K. Schaie, eds., *Life Span Developmental Psychology: Personality and Socialization* (New York: Academic Press, 1973), p. 202.

16. Ibid.

17. Carl Jung, *Modern Man in Search of a Soul* (New York: Harcourt, Brace & World, 1933), p. 264.

18. Erik Erikson, "Reflections on Dr. Borg's Life Cycle," *Daedalus* 105 (1976): 11.

19. Elisabeth Kübler-Ross, *On Death and Dying* (New York: Macmillan Co., 1969).

20. Readers might wish to consult Jeffrey Wicken's discussion of the importance of ecological concepts for bridging scientific, moral, and religious perspectives in his "Toward an Evolutionary Ecology of Meaning" in *Zygon* 24 (June, 1989): 153–184.

21. See Lawrence Kohlberg, *The Psychology of Moral Development* (San Francisco: Harper & Row, 1984) and *The Philosophy of Moral Development* (San Francisco: Harper & Row, 1981).

22. Lawrence Kohlberg, cited in Howard Munson's "Moral Thinking: Can It Be Taught?" *Psychology Today* (Feb., 1979): 53.

23. I have taken some liberty here in my interpretation of Kohlberg's findings. To be sure, Kohlberg insisted upon a formalistic definition of fully principled ethical thought by emphasizing the role of distinct formal cognitive operations such as reversibility. Yet, in "Continuities and Discontinuities" he acknowledges the functional/adaptive origin of such thought and its deep similarities to Erikson's notion of generativity. My point here is that implicit in Kohlberg's acknowledgment of the role of certain life tasks (such as giving sustained care to the next generation) in eliciting moral development is the recognition that it is indeed the interlocking web of human relationships that both prompts and structures fully mature moral thought.

24. Erikson, *Insight and Responsibility*, p. 233.

25. Ibid., p. 157.

Chapter 3
Philosophy and the Ethics of Care

1. Jeffrie Murphy, *Evolution, Morality, and the Meaning of Life* (Totowa, N.J.: Rowman & Littlefield, 1982), p. 73.

2. See William James, "Reflex Action and Theism," in *The Will to Believe* (New York: Dover Publications, 1956), pp. 111–144.

3. See William James, "The Sentiment of Rationality," in *Will to Believe,* pp. 63–110.

4. James, "Reflex Action," p. 114.

5. Ibid., p. 124.

6. Ibid., pp. 140 and 114.

7. Alfred North Whitehead, *The Function of Reason* (Boston: Beacon Press, 1956).

8. Herbert Spencer, cited in George Gaylord Simpson, *The Meaning of Evolution* (New Haven, Conn.: Yale University Press, 1949), p. 300.

9. William James, "The Moral Philosopher and the Moral Life," in *Will to Believe,* p. 195.

10. George Gaylord Simpson, *This View of Life* (New York: Harcourt, Brace & World, 1964), p. 105.

11. Antony Flew, *Evolutionary Ethics* (New York: Macmillan Co., 1967), p. 40.

12. William Frankena, *Ethics* (Englewood Cliffs, N.J.: Prentice-Hall, 1967), p. 77.

13. Lawrence Kohlberg, *The Philosophy of Moral Development* (San Francisco: Harper & Row, 1981), p. 121. Emphasis is mine.

14. Anthony Weston, "Beyond Intrinsic Value: Pragmatism in Environmental Ethics," *Environmental Ethics* 7 (Winter, 1985): 321.

15. James, "Moral Philosopher," p. 210.

16. Ibid., p. 211.

17. William James, *Psychology: The Briefer Course* (New York: Harper Torchbooks, 1961), p. 311.

18. See Don Browning, "William James's Philosophy of the Person: The Concept of the Strenuous Life," *Zygon* 10 (June, 1975): 162–174.

19. James, "Moral Philosopher," p. 212.

20. Ibid.

21. James, "Sentiment of Rationality," p. 75.

22. Browning, "William James's Philosophy of the Person," p. 172.

23. Robert Bellah, Richard Madsen, William Sullivan, Ann Swidler, and Steven Tipton, eds., *Habits of the Heart: Individualism and Commitment in American Life* (Berkeley, Calif.: University of California Press, 1985), p. 285.

24. William James, "On a Certain Blindness in Human Beings," in *Essays on Faith and Morals* (New York: Meridian Books, 1962), pp. 283–284.

25. C. Daniel Batson, "How Social an Animal?: The Human Capacity for Caring," *American Psychologist* 45 (March, 1990): 344.

Chapter 4
Caring as Participation in the Divine Life

1. Lawrence Kohlberg, "Continuities and Discontinuities in Childhood and Adult Moral Development Revisited," in R. Baltes and K. Schaie, eds., *Life Span Developmental Psychology: Personality and Socialization* (New York: Academic Press, 1973), p. 202.

2. Gordon Allport, *The Individual and His Religion* (New York: Macmillan & Co., 1950), p. 75.

3. This definition of religious thought is adapted from Don Browning's discussion of the relationship between theology and science in *Religious Thought and the Modern Psychologies* (Philadelphia: Fortress Press, 1987), p. 7.

4. William Clebsch, *American Religious Thought* (Chicago: University of Chicago Press, 1973), p. 2.

5. In his *Blessed Rage for Order* (New York: Seabury Press, 1975), David Tracy identifies the religious elements of existence in terms of what he calls the "limit dimension" of human experience, which refers to those situations in which people find themselves confronted with an ultimate limit or horizon to their experience. Such experiences occur in a variety of contexts. For example, such limits occur in scientific discourse whenever we contemplate the issue of the First Cause, when we consider teleological explanations of evolution, or when we try to make distinctions between material, efficient, and final causes. Limit experiences also underlie the majority of midlife developmental crises. There is also a pronounced limit dimension in a variety of psychological states such as those we associate with mysticism, conversion experience, peak experiences, etc. And, importantly, moral reflection also has a pronounced limit dimension insofar as it ultimately rests upon our ability to intuit the ultimate meaning or purpose of existence. For a more complete discussion of the various "limit experiences" confronted over the course of human development, readers might wish to consult my *Religion and the Life Cycle* (Philadelphia: Fortress Press, 1988).

6. This point needs to be qualified. Religious thought is, and rightfully should be, susceptible to the test of "pragmatic validation." Religious ideas arise in the same manner any other ideas arise in life. They are generated in the effort to adapt successfully to the various environments we inhabit and serve what might be called a guiding function in our practical lives. Those ideas that over time lead to successful modes of being in the world are, pragmatically considered, valid hypotheses about appropriate forms of conduct in life. Those that over time fail to connect with other known truths or fail to assist us in our lives are, pragmatically considered, either false or unimportant. Insofar as religious beliefs or practices appear to contribute to the objective and subjective richness of life, they rightfully

warrant our recognition as valuable "hypotheses" concerning the ultimate nature of reality. Even though the utility of a belief does not logically prove its truth, it does suggest that the belief in some way corresponds to the structure of reality and is worthy of our tentative acceptance.

7. Ernst Mayr, *The Growth of Biological Thought* (Cambridge, Mass.: Belknap Press, 1982), p. 81.

8. Arthur Peacocke, "Sociobiology and Its Theological Implications," *Zygon* 19 (June, 1984): 179.

9. Clebsch, *American Religious Thought*, p. xvi. Clebsch's claim that Jonathan Edwards, Ralph Waldo Emerson, and William James are the principal bearers of "a distinctively American spirituality" builds upon Perry Miller's important essay "From Edwards to Emerson," in which he argues that there is a strain of American spirituality that looks to "an indestructible element which was mystical, and a feeling for the universe which was almost pantheistic." See *Errand Into the Wilderness* (Cambridge, Mass.: Belknap Press, 1975).

10. Ralph Waldo Emerson, *The Complete Works of Ralph Waldo Emerson*, 12 vols. (New York: AMS Press, 1968), 1: 62.

11. Ibid.

12. Ralph Waldo Emerson, *The Early Lectures of Ralph Waldo Emerson*, 3 vols. (Cambridge, Mass.: Harvard University Press, 1959), 2: 89.

13. Ralph Waldo Emerson, *The Journals and Miscellaneous Notebooks of Ralph Waldo Emerson*, 14 vols. (Cambridge, Mass.: Harvard University Press, 1960), 4: 28.

14. Emerson, *Works*, 2: 282.

15. Emerson, *Journals*, 7: 450.

16. Emerson, *Works*, 1: 73.

17. See William James, "Essays in Radical Empiricism" in *Essays in Radical Empiricism and a Pluralistic Universe* (New York: E. P. Dutton, 1971). James also developed the philosophical foundations of radical empiricism in *The Varieties of Religious Experience* (New York: Collier Books, 1961) when he argued that "private and personal phenomena" constitute "realities in the completest sense of the term" (p. 386):

> A conscious field *plus* its object as felt or thought of *plus* an attitude towards the object *plus* the sense of a self to whom the attitude belongs—such a concrete bit of experience may be a small bit, but it is a solid bit as long as it lasts. . . . It is a *full* fact, even though it be an insignificant fact; it is of the *kind* to which all realities whatsoever must belong (p. 387).

18. James, *Varieties*, p. 399.

19. Gordon Kaufman, *Theology for a Nuclear Age* (Philadelphia: Westminster Press, 1985), p. 5. This entire section of ch. 4 follows Kaufman's cogent discussion of the need to rethink our conceptions of God and salvation in ways that illuminate our contemporary situation.

20. Ibid., p. 7.

21. Ibid., p. 35.

22. James argued quite persuasively against the tendency of many intellectuals to discredit religious belief because of its thoroughly nonscientific character. Conceding that religious beliefs do not have the status of factual truths in the sense that they lack demonstrable correspondence to objects already present in the outer environment, James nonetheless suggested that religious beliefs meet the criteria of rationality demanded by the functions of practical reason. Any philosophical perspective of truth that loses sight of the larger anthropological nature and function of reason is in danger of inventing epistemological criteria that are wholly lacking in anthropological validity. As James wrote in his famous essay "The Will to Believe," a "rule of thinking which would absolutely prevent me from acknowledging certain kinds of truth if these kinds of truth were really there, would be an irrational rule" (*The Will To Believe* [New York: Dover Publications, 1956], p. 28).

In this essay James convincingly demonstrates that our intellectual desire to "avoid error" can actually prevent us from "knowing the truth." In some instances belief in certain moral and religious ideas can create the truth of these ideas. He wrote, "There are, then, cases when a fact cannot come at all unless a preliminary faith exists in its coming. And where faith in a fact can help create the fact, that would be an insane logic which should say that faith running ahead of scientific evidence is the 'lowest kind of immorality' into which a thinking being can fall. Yet such is the logic by which our scientific absolutists pretend to regulate our lives" (p. 25).

23. William James, "Reflex Action and Theism," in *Will to Believe,* p. 126.

24. James, *Varieties,* p. 392.

25. James, *Pluralistic Universe,* p. 276.

26. Wendell Berry, *A Continuous Harmony* (New York: Harvest/Harcourt Brace Jovanovich, 1972), p. 6.

27. Ibid., p. 7.

28. James, *Pluralistic Universe,* p. 270. James adds here the interesting observation, "Let empiricism once become associated with religion, as hitherto, through some strange misunderstanding, it has been associated with irreligion, and I believe that a new era of religion as well as of philosophy will be ready to begin."

29. Ibid., p. 272.

30. Loren Eisley, *The Immense Journey* (New York: Vintage Books, 1957), p. 210.

31. Kaufman, *Theology for a Nuclear Age,* p. 43.

32. The three most important of Teilhard's books are *The Phenomenon of Man* (New York: Harper & Row, 1959), *The Divine Milieu* (New York: Harper & Row, 1965), and *Science and Christ* (New York: Harper & Row, 1965). Helpful expositions of Teilhard's thought can be found in Theodosius Dobzhansky's *The Biology of Ultimate Concern* (New York: Meridian Books, 1967), Philip Hefner's *The Promise of Teilhard* (Philadelphia: J. B. Lippincott Co.,

1970), and Robert Zaehner's *Evolution in Religion* (Oxford: Clarendon Press, 1971). Helpful critiques of the scientific status of Teilhard's writings include Theodosius Dobzhansky, "Teilhard and the Orientation of Evolution," *Zygon* 3 (Sept., 1968); Donald Genter, "The Scientific Basis of Some Concepts of Pierre Teilhard," *Zygon* 3 (Dec., 1968); George Riggan, "Testing the Teilhardian Foundations," *Zygon* 3 (Sept., 1968); and P. B. Medawar, "Critical Review of *The Phenomenon of Man*," *Mind* 70 (1961): 99–106.

33. John D. Barrow and Frank J. Tipler, *The Anthropic Cosmological Principle* (New York: Oxford University Press, 1988), p. 204.

34. James, *Varieties*, p. 406.

35. William James, cited in Clebsch, *American Religious Thought*, p. 168.

36. James, *Pluralistic Universe*, p. 272.

37. Ibid., p. 267.

38. Discussions of the psychological and cultural dimensions of narcissism can be found in Heinz Kohut, *The Search for the Self* (New York: International Universities Press, 1978), and Christopher Lasch, *The Culture of Narcissism* (New York: W. W. Norton & Co., 1970). A helpful discussion of the relationship between narcissism and modern religious life can be found in Donald Capps, "Religion and Psychological Well-Being," in Phillip E. Hammond, ed., *The Sacred in a Secular Age* (Berkeley, Calif.: University of California Press, 1985), pp. 237–256.

39. Kohut, *Search for the Self*, p. 459.

40. James, *Pluralistic Universe*, p. 267.

41. James, "Reflex Action and Theism," p. 127.

42. Kaufman, *Theology for a Nuclear Age*, p. 55.

43. James Lapsley presents a helpful account of a "process" interpretation of the Christian concept of salvation in his *Salvation and Health* (Philadelphia: Westminster Press, 1972).

44. Paul Tillich presents a suggestive model of how the various orders of existence participate in, and contribute to, the divine life in the third volume of his *Systematic Theology*, 3 vols. (Chicago: University of Chicago Press, 1967). Tillich replaces the conventional Christian conception of salvation with what he calls "essentialization," meaning the process by which "the new which has been actualized in time and space adds something to essential being, uniting it with the positive which is created within existence, thus producing the ultimately new, the 'New Being.' . . . Participation in the eternal life depends on a creative synthesis of a being's essential nature with what it has made of it in its temporal existence" (p. 400).

45. Kaufman, *Theology for a Nuclear Age*, p. 60.

46. Dobzhansky, *Biology of Ultimate Concern*, p. 136.

47. Teilhard, *Phenomenon of Man*, p. 246.

48. Teilhard, cited in Dobzhansky, *Biology of Ultimate Concern*, p. 137.

49. Kaufman, *Theology for a Nuclear Age*, p. 58.

50. Jeffrey Wicken, "Toward an Evolutionary Ecology of Meaning," *Zygon* 24 (June, 1989): 103.

Conclusion:
Care, Commitment, and the Cure of Souls

1. Clifford Geertz, *The Interpretation of Cultures* (New York: Basic Books, 1973), p. 52.

2. Ibid., p. 90.

3. Ibid., p. 112. Emphasis is mine.

4. The most eloquent chronicle of this crisis in American culture is *Habits of the Heart: Individualism and Commitment in American Life,* ed. Robert Bellah, Richard Madsen, William Sullivan, Ann Swidler, and Steven M. Tipton (Berkeley, Calif.: University of California Press, 1985).

5. See Philip Rieff, *The Triumph of the Therapeutic: Uses of Faith After Freud* (New York: Harper & Row, 1966).

6. Philip Rieff, *Freud: The Mind of the Moralist* (New York: Doubleday & Co., Anchor Books, 1961), p. 391.

7. Robert Pirsig, *Zen and the Art of Motorcycle Maintenance* (New York: William Morrow & Co., 1974), from the preface.

8. Ibid., p. 290.

9. Ibid., p. 352.

10. See John T. McNeill, *A History of the Cure of Souls* (New York: Harper & Row, 1951).

11. Charles Jaekle and William Clebsch, *Pastoral Care in Historical Perspective* (New York: Jason Aronson, 1975).

12. Robert C. Fuller, *Religion and the Life Cycle* (Philadelphia: Fortress Press, 1988).

13. See Paul Tillich's discussion of the correlational method in his *Systematic Theology,* vol. 1 (Chicago: University of Chicago Press, 1951), David Tracy's revision of this method in his *Blessed Rage for Order* (New York: Seabury Press, 1975) and "The Foundations of Practical Theology" in Don Browning, ed., *Pastoral Theology* (San Francisco: Harper & Row, 1983), and Don Browning's contributions to a revised correlational method in "Mapping the Terrain of Pastoral Theology: Toward a Practical Theology of Care," in *Pastoral Psychology* 36 (Fall, 1987): 10–28 and *Religious Thought and the Modern Psychologies: A Critical Conversation in the Theology of Culture* (Philadelphia: Fortress Press, 1987).

14. Don Browning, *The Moral Context of Pastoral Care* (Philadelphia: Westminster Press, 1976), p. 103.

Index

✳

Tillich, Paul, 103, 117nn47–48
Tipler, Frank, 87
Tracy, David, 103, 108n3

variation and evolutionary change, 17

Weston, Anthony, 68
Whitehead, Alfred North, 62, 85
Wicken, Jeffrey, 93–94
Wilson, Edward O., 21, 25, 28
Winnicott, D. W., 32

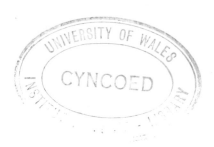